EXCELLENCE IN EDUCATION PUBLICATIONS

BUSINESS ENGLISH U.S.A.

A Textbook of American Business English, Culture, Etiquette, and Business Planning for Students of English as a Second Language

MICHAEL F. SUDLOW

MA – Brigham Young University

AARON P. GROW

MA – Colorado State University

BUSINESS ENGLISH U.S.A.

Publishing:	*Excellence In Education Publications* Salt Lake City, Utah · Monmouth, Oregon
Edited By:	Roger Shinkle
Illustrations:	Rudy Bischof
Design & Layout:	Marc Neidlinger
Printing & Binding:	MC Printing of Provo, Utah U.S.A.

ISBN   1-8-77-591-08-4

First edition:	November 1981
Second Edition:	June 1987
Third Edition:	June 1988
Fourth Edition:	November 1993
Fifth Edition:	April 1998

TABLE OF CONTENTS

continued

TABLE OF CONTENTS

continued. . .

TABLE OF CONTENTS

SECTION 5 - English in the Workplace

The Office Worker

The Factory Worker

A Worker's Life

continued. . .

T A B L E O F C O N T E N T S

TO THE STUDENT

As a student of English, you will be glad to hear that this second edition of *Business English USA* has been specifically designed with you in mind. As you use *Business English USA*, make sure you take full advantage of every single page of information in this book. All of the business, culture and etiquette ideas and related vocabulary that are in this text are presented in such a way as to be used with teacher assistance to be easily understood. and quickly learned.

We realize, however, that simply reading this textbook will probably not be enough to fully understand and remember the information. A more sure way to remember the information and related vocabulary given in this book will be to actively use it. This is why you will find a number of exercises and activities placed throughout every chapter. As you study each lesson, make it a priority to work on these parts of the chapters. We firmly believe that the more you actively "do," the more you will learn.

To emphasize this point of view, you will find that the final sections of this second edition of *Business English USA* are also designed for your specific involvement. The final two sections of this text include key components of a standard business plan, a plan which your teacher may or may not have you work on as an integral part of the course. Every chapter of this text relates directly to certain aspects of doing business. As you learn about each new business topic, you can turn to the related part in the final two sections and complete them for yourself as you put together plans for your very own enterprise.

Our goal in developing this text was to provide a textbook which not only provides the standard vocabulary and concepts necessary to operate effectively in English speaking business environments, but to present the material in an enjoyable and memorable way. It is our hope that as you study from *Business English USA* you will find these two goals to be met to your satisfaction as you continue to pursue your own personal business interests in the future.

TO THE TEACHER

Of the several books which Excellence in Education has available, we are proud to say that *Business English USA* is one of the most popular. We would like to think that this is no accident. Your selection of this book for your Business English class will be rewarded in several ways.

First of all, you will quickly see that *Business English USA* is one of the most versatile ESP texts on the market. Each chapter contains an area of information and vocabulary salient to specific areas of business in America. Each chapter could be studied in isolation. Using this text as a resource, teachers can work with only those sections that interest them and their students in meeting class goals.

For teachers who prefer to follow the topical organization of this text in the teaching of classes, this second edition of *Business English USA* offers two possibilities. First, students can be guided through each chapter from beginning to end to study the information contained within each unit. Second, on top of the first option, teachers can also utilize the Business Plan Assignments (located on each assignment page) and the Business Plan Section (at the end of the book). We feel that having students actually create their own business plans is one of the best ways they will retain the information and vocabulary found on the pages of this book.

Even though we are very pleased with the information given in this text. It will also be evident in using Business English USA that we strongly encourage the use of materials found in the "real world" as well. Examples of this sentiment are found in assignments which have students read from actual business magazines or search for information in actual phone books and classified ads. Gather and use all of the phone books, magazines, memos, newsletters and newspapers you can so that when this ESP course is over, your students will be able to delve into and decipher these types of materials on their own.

It is in the accomplishing of this goal that we feel the most satisfaction; to teach students how to teach themselves!

One final note. To add a bit of humor to the text a fictional company known as Boromoke (pronounced, boh-row-mo-kay) is featured throughout this book. Boromoke is a Japanese term for "rip-off" or "undiscovered profit."

We hope you enjoy using Business English U.S.A.

SECTION 1

Creating Your Own Business Plan

CREATING YOUR OWN BUSINESS PLAN
INTRODUCTION

Throughout this text you will have the opportunity to put together a Business Plan component by component. At the end of each lesson, you will be given tasks to complete. By the time you complete the text, you will have a complete business plan for a business you design from scratch.

There are many very practical reasons for developing a business plan. The first and perhaps most obvious reason is that if you wish to request a loan from a bank, the bank will require that you show them one. A second reason for creating a business plan is that it helps you, the entrepreneur, express to yourself and others just exactly what it is that you intend to do as well as why, how, and when. If a business plan is carefully developed, it will be very clear whether or not the business you are thinking of should even be started.

As you do the tasks outlined on the Assignment Pages of each lesson, remember that completeness and neatness count. Put yourself in the place of a loan officer. Would you loan money to a person who does not do things as professionally as possible? For this reason, it is suggested that as you complete each task, you place the end product, the chart, drawings, and other information in a well-organized format, in a three-ring binder, along with a cover page, table of contents, and a pocket to include larger items related to the project.

After all the tasks are completed, you will have an opportunity to orally present your business plan to the class or to the teacher. You will be asked to prepare copies of your report for the teacher and the other class members.

After reading each component, do the assigned task. Now, let's get started!

Note to the teacher: *This Business Plan can be completed as part of each lesson or as a totally independent project. Working with the students, determine how you would like to have them work on this project.*

LIST OF TASKS

The components of the business plan will be presented in the following order:

Task #	Name of Task
Task #1	Complete a Market Survey
Task #2	Identify Your Target Audience
Task #3	Create a Mission Statement
Task #4	Determine a Location
Task #5	Calculate Your Cash Flow
Task #6	Establish a Time Line
Task #7	Develop an Advertising and Marketing Plan
Task #8	Design and Get Estimates for Name-Carrying Materials
Task #9	Prepare to Hire & Train New Employees
Task #10	Hang Out Your Shingle
Task #11	Present Your Business Plan

COMPLETE A MARKET SURVEY

Before going too deep into a new business venture, it is very important to complete a market survey. You will need to find out if there is a need for your business in your immediate area and what kind of competition is already out there.

As you do your research, find out as much as you can about the success/failure ratio of similar businesses, especially in the area you want to work in. Ask yourself and others what the future of such a business might be. Try to see how economic, social, and technological trends might affect the future of your new business.

If possible, find out as much as possible about the business from people already in the field. Because your competitors will not want to give you a lot of information, you may have to go to another city or area to speak to people in the same business field.

If you haven't chosen a location, get information from the local Chamber of Commerce and look in the local Yellow Pages to see what kind of competition already exists in the area.

Your purpose of this market survey is to learn in a systematic, unbiased way whether or not your proposed business is a viable one. By heavily researching these questions at the very beginning of your project, you could save yourself countless hours of time (and possibly thousands of dollars!) down the road.

Your Tasks:

1)   Using the Yellow Pages of the phone book, find out how many competitors there are in your area. Call them and ask how long they have been in business.

2)   Prepare a questionnaire (market survey) to have an unbiased person ask at least 100 people in the area you hope to locate in. Ask the following types of questions:

         a)   Do you think there is a need for a (type of business) in this area? Yes, No

         b)   Why?

         c)   How often do you use the services of (this type of business)?

         d)   Where do you go now for this service?

         e)   How much do you normally spend in a month at (this type of business)?

3)   Compile the results of the survey. If there is a definite need for the proposed business and potential for success, continue to Task #2. If your market survey shows that your business will probably fail, choose a new business and redo Task #1.

IDENTIFY YOUR TARGET AUDIENCE

Who will your customers be? Young people? Families? Senior citizens? The general population? Will your clients come primarily from your own city or from a wider area? Will you need to prepare to advertise locally, in a wide region, or even on the Internet?

Along with the need to identify where your customers will be coming from, one of the most important factors to consider is how many customers you will realistically have.

Information regarding location of customers will depend heavily on the type of business you open. For example, if you open a local restaurant, your customers will mostly come from the immediate area. If you are getting into a more specialized field, your customers could come from far away and may have learned about you through the Internet or a mail-order catalog.

You will need to determine if your target audience is going to be growing or at least stable. If it is going to become smaller, perhaps you need to consider a different business venture.

Countless businesses have been started by people who saw a need for a product or service. Will yours be such a business?

Your Tasks:

    1)   Make a list of the type of people you hope will make up your customer base.

    2)   Decide how you would like to reach the target audience. Newspaper ads? The Yellow Pages? The Internet? Radio ads?

    3)   Make a one-page Yellow Page ad.

CREATE A MISSION STATEMENT

With an idea of the market potential and target audience, you are ready to decide exactly what your new business venture will actually do. You are ready to write a Mission Statement, a short, concise statement that describes the purpose of your company.

The more specific you are in writing your company's mission statement, the more guidance you will give yourself when it comes time to make decisions regarding the way the business should go.

Naturally, in time a company's mission statement may change. For example, a new candy store may want to sell candy locally and to be the best-selling candy store in the area. That company's mission statement might be something like, "To provide the best candy in the city at the best price." But what would happen if the candy became world famous? The new mission statement might read, "Our mission is to become the largest candy manufacturer in the world and to provide the finest candy to customers around the world."

In short, a mission statement helps its writer(s) set their sights on an agreed goal, making many of the future business decisions easier to address.

Your Task:

> Write a mission statement for your company.
> Be concise in describing exactly what you intend your company to do and achieve.

DETERMINE A LOCATION

Depending on the business that you're in, the actual location that you choose to set up your business could be one of the most important choices you make. This is particularly true if you are involved in any kind of business that requires customers to physically come into your establishment to do business, such as a restaurant or a store.

If your business is service oriented and goes out to customers, there can be more flexibility in where the business is located.

To help locate a site, it is recommended that a local real estate agent be involved. A real estate agent is a professional who can help you determine whether you need to purchase, lease, rent, or perhaps build a building.

Whether you rent or buy your place of business will depend upon several factors including:

available capital	the neighborhood
ease of access and parking	property taxes
maintenance	utility costs
room for future expansion, etc.	

Your Tasks:

1) Determine the site you will select as your business location. On a single sheet of paper write down the address and four or five main reasons you feel the site you have chosen is the best for your business.

2) Include an area map or drawing showing the streets and other businesses in the same local area.

3) Write down the monthly costs associated with the site (building). What will the monthly lease, rent, or mortgage be? What will the cost of utilities, taxes, maintenance, insurance, etc. be? Add up these costs and multiply by 12 to see what the yearly location costs will be. (Estimates are OK in areas where students are unable to do actual research.)

CALCULATE YOUR CASH FLOW

It is at this point that you need to begin to think very specifically about the products and/or services you will offer. There are many ways you can do this. Perhaps one of the best methods is to use a data sheet approach. A data sheet method requires the future business person to list every conceivable expense of the company as well as projected profits of the first year.

A fact sheet such as this will also include a listing of all employees (including yourself) needed at the time of start-up. Often there is only an owner doing all the work at this point, but it is important to budget for other necessary helpers. You will also need to estimate costs of necessary supplies and inventory. Don't forget such items as stationery, envelopes, checks, receipts, business cards, and other such items.

After you have added up all of these figures plus an additional 10% emergency fund, ask yourself if you have enough start-up capital or if you need a bank loan to get started. If you plan on applying for a bank loan, you will be required to provide the bank with as much detail as possible.

The most important trick to successfully starting a new business is to never, never run out of cash! Remember, too, that your expenses will almost always be more than you estimated and your income will often be less than you thought.

Please remember Murphy's Law, "If anything can go wrong, it will go wrong."

Your Task:

> Create a cash flow data sheet which itemizes all expenses for the first year of operation. Remember to include all costs as explained above. Then estimate how much income you will realistically make through sales of your products or services.

ESTABLISH A TIME LINE

Now it is time to make a time line or dates by which you hope things will happen. Such items on your time line will include:

> finding a suitable location
> obtaining all necessary licenses and government paperwork
> applying for and obtaining a loan
> purchasing furnishings and equipment for the location
> installation of signs, phone lines, etc.
> projected opening or starting date
> deadline for hiring and training new employees
> advertising schedule (how often and where will ads run)
> announcement of opening
> etc.

If you are unsure of what other things to consider, contact the Small Business Administration and ask for free information on how to start up a new business.

Your Task:

> Develop a realistic time line of when you intend to actually start your business. Using dates as benchmarks, list all of the things you will need to do, buy, and take care of between now and then.

DEVELOP AN ADVERTISING AND MARKETING PLAN

Another key aspect of any successful business venture is the quality and the quantity of the advertising that gets done. There are many professionals available for you to consult in this area. And for those who are computer literate, there are many programs available for desk top publishers that will help you make professional looking ads.

It is important to match the type of advertising you will do with the particular audience you intend to cater to. Of course, this will already be established based on previous research. Will your ads and marketing have a comical bend to possibly attract a more youthful group? Or will they take on the more serious and professional tone used in trying to attract a more mature audience?

Remember, there are many different ways of advertising that can be used. Print media includes magazines, newspapers, or direct mailings. Mass media involves the use of television or radio. Many times it is your budget that will decide what type of advertising and how many ads you will be able to run. However, name recognition will be an important goal for your new business.

Basically there are three areas in which all businesses compete and try to make themselves stand out from their competitors: service, quality, and price. No matter what they sell, they must stand out in one or more of these areas. Decide what areas you will compete in and promote your business accordingly.

Your Tasks:

Develop the marketing strategy that you will use to promote your business.

1)   Design (or have someone help you design) a quarter page ad for a newspaper or magazine that you would use to promote your new business.

2)   Develop a company slogan or motto to use in your advertisements and printed material.

3)   Design a logo to be used on any printed material.

4)   Write a 30-second radio ad that you can use to let people know about your new business.

5)   Estimate the costs of your advertising budget for your first year.

DESIGN AND GET ESTIMATES FOR NAME-CARRYING MATERIALS

Most entrepreneurs design their logos, name cards, and stationery long before completing other tasks in planning a business. In fact, it is sometimes the creation of these items that provides the push to actually go through with putting together a complete company.

Although there is nothing wrong with creating these items first, it might be a better idea to wait until most other plans have been taken care of before actually going to a print shop to get your name-carrying materials printed up.

Similar to the advertising campaign that you decide upon, the design of your letterhead, business cards, logo, and company sign should also reflect the tone of the business you plan to operate. Generally, however, no matter what your business is, the higher the quality of these materials, the more regard people will give your business.

Your Tasks:

    1)   On a clean sheet of paper, (and using a word processor if possible), design the type of letterhead you wish to use in your business. Be sure to use your new logo on the letterhead. Find out the cost of printing 500 sheets on high quality paper.

    2)   Design a name card and get a cost estimate for 500 cards.

PREPARE TO HIRE AND TRAIN NEW EMPLOYEES

Although most of what a person needs for a job will be learned on the job, you will need people who can be trained to do the job the way you want it done. If your new employees will be dealing directly with your customers, it is important to hire employees with good people skills.

If you need people with bookkeeping skills, a pleasant telephone voice, sales experience, or other talents, you will need to place help wanted ads in the newspaper, set up an interview schedule, and prepare the paperwork for hiring new employees.

And as much as possible, make a list of all the duties each new employee is expected to perform. Employees will also want to know what their basic pay will be, what benefits they will receive, their working hours, vacation days, and other work-related information.

Your Tasks:

1)   Make a list of the employees you absolutely need. Then list their duties under each job title.

2)   Write up a Help Wanted ad to place in the newspaper to find people for these positions.

3)   Prepare a job application form to be used in interviewing potential new employees.

4)   Calculate the costs of paying each new employee. Add approximately 10% above their base pay to cover various government taxes. For example, if you pay a person $6.50 an hour, calculate that your costs will be $7.15 per hour.

HANG OUT YOUR SHINGLE

In years past, the only thing that was really necessary to open a business was a special skill or talent and a place to do it. Once a person had these two things, all they had left to do was put up a shingle (sign) outside their office or location to let others know that they were now in business.

Nowadays, as you have seen through these various tasks, there is a lot more to starting a business than that. Every step in creating this business plan has been intended to help you succeed in your venture with a minimum amount of risk. If all previous tasks have gone smoothly, it is time to open your doors. Make it official by placing an ad and your telephone number in the phone book. If possible, get a telephone number that spells part of your name. For example, if you open a book store, your telephone number might be 838-BOOK (838-2665) making it easy for people to remember your number.

Your Tasks:

    1)   Make up a customized phone number and an ad to be placed in the Yellow Pages.

    2)   Design a company sign to be located outside the building.

PRESENT YOUR BUSINESS PLAN

Now that you have finished compiling all the information for your business plan, prepare to present it to the class. Remember, neatness counts. Make your presentation as professional as possible.

Your tasks:

1) Make a bound copy of your business plan for yourself, your teacher, and other class members (if required by your teacher).

2) On your assigned date, be prepared to make a 30-minute to one-hour presentation to the class on your new business plan.

3) Be prepared to answer questions and provide facts and figures for the teacher and other students regarding your plan.

SECTION 2

Getting Started In Business Situations

This introductory section of *Business English: USA* will help you get started on the road to a successful business relationship with your present and future American clients. We will guide you through a step-by-step process and give you valuable advice regarding etiquette and business customs. In this lesson you will study the following:

Establishing Contact with Clients

Appointment Do's and Don'ts

Phoning an Unknown Client

Introducing Yourself and Others

Meeting Clients for the First Time

Small Talk with a New Client

Inviting a Client to Lunch & Declining an Invitation

Hosting a Business Lunch

Body Language

Before going to the United States on business, it is important to establish contact with your potential clients. There are several important steps to follow.

KENKO INDUSTRIES
38-24-36 BIMBO DORI
CHIIYODA-KU, TOKYO 183
JAPAN

PHONE: (03) 5325-6628 · *FAX:* (03) 5325-6629
E-mail: ken@jol.com

June 24, 1999

Mr. Jeff Nielson, Mgr.
Import & Marketing Dept.
HONEST TRADERS, LTD.
1001 Sunset Blvd.
Hollywood, CA 90158
USA

Dear Mr. Nielson:

We learned of your firm through the magazine *American Importer*. We would like to introduce ourselves to you.

Since our founding in 1953, Kenko Industries has become one of the leading manufacturers and distributors of plastic items in the Far East. We have earned a reputation for high quality and price competitiveness with our products as evidenced by our high sales growth.

Having attained great success here in the markets of the Far East, we would like to offer our products to the United States market. Because of your excellent reputation as an importer and distributor, we would like to see you on our visit to the United States. We will be in your area September 15-20, and would like to know when it would be convenient to meet with you.

We have enclosed our brochure and catalog. Please feel free to ask any questions you may have. Thank you for your time; we look forward to hearing from you soon.

Sincerely,
KENKO INDUSTRIES

Kennichi Shiraishi
Sales Manager
Export Department

KS:pt
Enclosure: catalog / brochure

1) Send a letter of introduction by mail, fax, or e-mail. Let them know how you received their name. Tell who you are and why you are writing.

State that you would be interested in setting up an appointment on a suggested date.

Let them know that you will be waiting for a reply.

2) Wait for a reply.

3) Write a follow-up letter if an answer has been received. Confirm the date and time. Ask for directions to the company.

4) Confirm your appointment before you depart.

5) Make contact by telephone before going to the appointment.

Basic Rules to Remember

1) Keep the letter short.

2) Avoid using formal words.

3) Enclose or send informational literature (brochures, catalogs, etc).

APPOINTMENT DO'S AND DONT'S

After arriving at your destination, reconfirm your appointment by telephone. Study the list of do's and don'ts below to make the best possible first impression at your appointment.

1) Arrive to your appointment on time.

2) If you are going to be late, telephone immediately and inform the client of the fact.

3) If it is necessary to cancel your appointment, telephone at once and explain the circumstances as simply as possible. Arrange a new time if the situation permits.

4) Rise to meet anyone coming into the office: male or female.

5) Dress neatly and be presentable.

6) Shake hands firmly.

7) As foreign names are often difficult to pronounce and remember, give a business card to those with whom you are meeting and say your name slowly and clearly.

8) If your contact is speaking too fast or using vocabulary that is too difficult for you, don't be embarrassed to ask him to speak more slowly or more simply. Remember, your contacts want to make a business deals that will be beneficial to them in some way or they wouldn't be meeting with you.

9) In a business meeting, it is impolite to speak in a language that not everyone understands. If more than one native language is spoken in your group, discuss everything in English, even among yourselves, so that all may understand.

10) Be frank! Americans don't like people to "beat around the bush."

There may be times when you receive "leads" from clients or colleagues for possible future customers. You should always take advantage of these leads if you are in the area by phoning, even if you have not contacted that person by letter beforehand.

PHONING AN UNKNOWN CLIENT

Receptionist: Mid-East Plastics Company. May I help you?

Mr. Kim: Hello. My name is Kim, Tae-Hyun of Kensong Industries in Seoul, Korea. I would like to speak to someone regarding our line of plastic products, please.

Receptionist: I'll connect you with our products manager, Mr. Al-Sanna. Hold, please.

Al-Sanna: Hamad Al-Sanna. May I help you?

Mr. Kim: Hello Mr. Al-Sanna. My name is Kim, Tae-Hyun of Kensong Industries in Seoul, Korea. We manufacture plastic products. I heard through George Nebeker of B & S Company that you are a leading distributor of plastic products. I was wondering if I could see you sometime tomorrow morning to introduce our line to you.

Al-Sanna: Yes, I would be very interested. Would tomorrow morning at 10:00 be all right?

Mr. Kim: Yes, that would be fine. Can you tell me how to get to your office from the Hollywood Holiday Inn?

CLIENT NOT IN

Receptionist: Mr. Al-Sanna's office.

Mr. Kim: Hello. May I speak to Mr. Al-Sanna please?

Receptionist: I'm sorry, he's out at the moment. May I take a message?

Mr. Kim: Yes. My name is Kim, Tae-Hyun of Kensong Industries in Seoul, Korea. We are a manufacturer of plastic products; I wanted to see Mr. Al-Sanna so I could introduce our line to him. Can you tell me when he will be in?

Receptionist: He should be back around 2:00 this afternoon.

Mr. Kim: Thank you very much. I'll call back again at 2:00.

Receptionist: I'll tell him you called. Thank you for calling.

Mr. Kim: Thank you. Goodbye.

ASSIGNMENT: *After discussing these dialogues with your teacher, pair up with a partner and practice them in class. Be sure to use information from your own company as well as your own name.*

INTRODUCING YOURSELF AND OTHERS

Introductions are an important part of any business meeting. Let's study the various ways you can introduce yourself and others.

1) When meeting someone for the first time, the following phrases are commonly used:

    a) "How do you do?"(This is not actually a question.)   d) "(It's) nice to meet you."
    b) "(It's) a pleasure to meet you."   e) "(I'm) happy to meet you."
    c) "(I'm) glad to meet you."

2) Upon leaving or departing, these phrases are commonly used:

    a) "(It was) nice meeting you."   d) "(It was) nice to meet you."
    b) "(It was) nice to have met you."   e) "(I'm) happy to have met you."
    c) "(I'm) glad to have met you."   f) "(It was) a pleasure meeting you."

    NOTE: the verb *to meet* is used when seeing someone for the first time. If meeting someone a second or third time, the verb *to see* is used and the word *again* is added to the sentence. If you use the verb *to meet* with a person you know, it is absolutely necessary to add *again*.

    EXAMPLE: "I'm happy to see you again."   OR   "It's nice to meet you again."

3) In the United States and many western cultures, there is not a big distinction between people because of age, occupation, or income. Nevertheless, there are a few points to remember:

    a)   If you are introducing yourself, here are two phrases to use:
            1) "How do you do? I'm Richard Bruggermann." (more formal)
            2) "Hello. I'm Mr. Bruggermann." (less formal)

    b)   Do not introduce yourself by your last name only.
            EXAMPLE: "I'm Bruggermann."

    c)   When introducing other people, always show respect to clients, senior executives, important guests, and VIPs by stating their names first.
            EXAMPLE: "Mr. Cardon (your company president), this is Michael Jamison, the new supply clerk."

    d)   If you are introducing a man and a woman, the man is presented to the woman first.
            EXAMPLE: "Miss Pickering, this is Mr. Adachi."

MEETING CLIENTS FOR THE FIRST TIME

You are now in your first meeting with a potential new client. Here are a few important things to remember when meeting a business client for the first time.

1)   Make eye contact. Try not to appear nervous (even if you are!).

2)   If your hands feel sweaty, simply wipe off your right hand as you extend it to shake hands. A wet, sweaty handshake does not leave a good impression.

3)   Stand straight. Do not bow while shaking hands.

4)   Shake hands firmly. Never shake hands like a "dead fish."

5)   Wait until after you shake hands to present your business card. In many American business situations, the business card is presented at the end of a presentation or discussion. However, to help the client understand how to pronounce your name or to learn more about you and your position, exchanging cards at the beginning would be appropriate.

SMALL TALK WITH A NEW CLIENT

After introductions have been made, your client will invite you to sit down. In case he doesn't, always ask "May I sit down?" before sitting.

Your client will usually be the first to talk. He might ask you a question or make a comment on a subject other than business. This could be about the weather ("It's been rather warm lately") or about you ("Is this your first visit to the United States?"). It is important that you try to carry the conversation with questions and comments that will lead to a real conversation (not just "Yes" and "No" responses).

Below is a sample conversation.

Mr. Heim:	Please sit down. (or Please have a seat.)
Mr. Silva:	Thank you, Mr. Heim.
Mr. Heim:	Please call me Steve. May I call you Alex?[1]
Mr. Silva:	By all means.
Mr. Heim:	Is this your first time in Los Angeles, Alex?
Mr. Silva:	Yes. This is my first time here, but I have been to Miami and New York before.
Mr. Heim:	Oh! Was it on business or pleasure?
Mr. Silva:	A little of both. Have you ever been to Brazil, Steve?
Mr. Heim:	No, but I'd love to go. I've always wanted to see the Carnival. If we get some business going, maybe I will have the chance to go to Brazil.
Mr. Silva:	I hope so. Well, I know you are busy.[2] May I show you what we can offer you?
Mr. Heim:	Please do.

Notes:

1   Americans enjoy doing business on a "first name basis." If your name is long and hard to pronounce or remember, you may want to shorten it or use a nickname.

2   If you don't have much time, you can cut short the informal conversation and move right into the business presentation by saying, " I know you are busy so I will tell you why I wanted to see you today."

INVITING A CLIENT TO LUNCH (By Phone)

You may want to invite a client to lunch where you can meet in a less formal setting than in an office. This is a good chance to develop a relationship of trust and confidence with the new client. Below are two dialogues which will be useful in making and declining invitations.

Boromoke:	Hello. Boromoke Corporation. May I help you?
Mr. Kim:	Yes, this is Mr. Kim of the Kim Chee Company. May I speak to Mr. Cook, please?
Boromoke:	One moment please. I'll connect you.
Mr. Cook:	Hello Mr. Kim. How are you doing?
Mr. Kim:	Great. Say, I was wondering if we could get together for lunch tomorrow. I have an interesting proposal I'd like to present to you.
Mr. Cook:	Sounds great. Where shall we meet?
Mr. Kim:	How about the "Ghengis Khan Barbecue Restaurant" on 9th Avenue at 12:00?
Mr. Cook:	That will be fine. Thanks for calling.
Mr. Kim:	See you tomorrow at twelve.

DECLINING AN INVITATION

Bandana:	Good morning. Bandana Banana Company. May I help you?
Mr. Gomez:	Hello. This is Eduardo Gomez of the Barrato Shipping Company. Is Mr. Castro in?
Bandana:	Yes, he is. Just a moment; I'll ring his extension.
Castro:	Hello Eduardo. How's business?
Mr. Gomez:	Not bad. Say, I was wondering if you'd like to join me for lunch tomorrow? There's a friend of mine in town I'd like you to meet.
Castro:	Oh, that's too bad. I really appreciate the invitation, but I'm tied up all day tomorrow. Could I take a raincheck for the day after tomorrow?
Mr. Gomez:	No problem. I'll call you later with details of the time and place.
Castro:	Thanks for calling, Ed. I'll be waiting to hear from you.

HOSTING A BUSINESS LUNCH

Hosting a business lunch is a great way to start or continue a business discussion. Business lunches are held between the hours of 11:30 and 2:30 and last a maximum of one and a half hours. First names are used at these informal meetings.

If hosting a business lunch, remember the following points:

1) Be on time. Don't keep your guests waiting.

2) When you enter the restaurant, the woman guest should enter first. A male host would hold the door open for her upon entering and leaving the restaurant.

3) Inside the restaurant, the Maitre d' will normally guide the guests to the table and will often help the woman into her seat. If he doesn't, the host, or another male guest, should ask her if he can hold her chair. If other women are present, each man should ask to help the woman nearest him with her coat and into her seat. The woman is always seated first.

4) When you are seated and have ordered, don't jump right into a business discussion. Even if you have something important to discuss, save it until after eating (or once dessert is served) or until your client brings it up. The lunch is for getting to know each other on a personal basis.

5) Drink alcohol cautiously! You may have just finished a successful business agreement which calls for celebration. American business people do not usually drink alcohol at lunch time, so if you do suggest a drink, limit yourself to one or two drinks. You might say, "Well, I don't usually drink this early, but today calls for a celebration."

6) If you have made the invitation, you, as the host, should suggest the most expensive item on the menu. This will let the guests know that they can order whatever they like.

7) If the business lunch was a mutual decision, it is best that one party "treat" the other rather than "splitting the bill." Your client may insist on paying, but if he doesn't, you should say "This is on me " or " This is my treat. "

Note: Some women, especially those in business, do not care for special treatment. It is perfectly acceptable for a woman to seat herself or to pay if she desires.

8) When the meal is completed, quietly ask for the check.

9) After paying the bill and arranging for the tip, the host announces the end of the luncheon by standing up. The men should help the women with their chairs and their coats.

10) The host leaves last.

BODY LANGUAGE

Many times we make a bigger impression not by what we say, but by our physical actions. These actions are called our "Body Language." On the following two pages, you will find short explanations of how we "speak" without speaking and the good or bad impressions such actions may give to those around us.

HANDSHAKES VS. BOWING
Some foreign business people have a tendency to bow while shaking hands. This is not a good practice. It is important to look a Westerner in the eye when shaking hands. Second, it is important to shake hands firmly. Too often businesspeople shake hands very weakly or half-handedly. A handshake is often a way to judge a person's character. A handshake can leave a good impression or a bad one. How well do you shake hands?

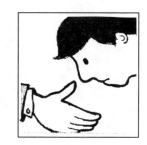

WALKING BETWEEN PEOPLE
In some countries when a person has to walk between people, it is common to see that person move his hand in an up and down chopping motion as he walks through. In the west, this practice is meaningless. When a person needs to walk between two people (if there is no other way around), he only needs to say, "Excuse me" and proceed through. The road blockers should apologize for being in the way. Show us how to walk between people in your country.

BUMPING INTO PEOPLE
Because of the crowded conditions in public places in some cities and some countries, it is not uncommon to push and bump into people all day long without apologizing in any way. In most places in the west, however, anytime one person bumps into or is bumped by someone else, both parties (the bumper and bumpee) should apologize immediately. The bumper should emphasize the *me* in "Excuse me."

WHO ME?
In the United States when people point to themselves and say "Who me?" they point to their chests. What do you point at in your country?

NO THANK YOU
To non-verbally indicate "No thank you," Americans shake or move their heads in a left-right sideways motion. Sometimes they put one hand up at about head level with the palm facing the speaker. How do you indicate "no thank you" non-verbally in your country?

BODY LANGUAGE

COME HERE

Americans use a different way to motion for a person to "come here" than do most other people in the world. Americans close the hand, raise the index finger with the front of the hand facing themselves and move the index finger back and forth. Waving the hand up and down with the arm extended means "goodbye."
How do you signal "come here" and "goodbye" in your country?

OK

When the thumb and the index finger are formed to make a circle, it means "OK." In some countries it means "money" and in some South American countries it has a very bad meaning and should be avoided. What does this symbol mean in your country?

THUMBS UP

Closing the fist and raising the thumb skyward signifies "OK" or approval. Pointing the thumb downward indicates disapproval. The phrase "thumbs up" is used in speech to indicate the same as the hand signal. And of course, "thumbs down" means "I disapprove." Now, is it thumbs up or thumbs down to your English teacher? The thumb is also used in hitchhiking to indicate which direction the hitchhiker wants to go.

COME ON!

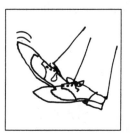

If a person is tired of waiting or impatient, he will often stamp the front end of one foot rhythmically or drum the fingers of one hand with the heel of the hand on a desk or something firm. This indicates to the other person that he is anxious to get going or tired of waiting.

WHAT'S IN A WINK?

A wink can have many meanings to Americans. If you like a person of the opposite sex, you can wink at that person. It is a symbol to show that you are interested in getting to know that person better. Another meaning of a wink is that you were just kidding. In such a case, the wink comes right after the joke.

SECTION 3

English In Communications

COMMUNICATIONS
Phone, Faxes, & E-mail

Phones

Answering Machine	Conference Call	Push Button Phone
Area Code	Country (City) Code	Rates
Automatic Redial	Direct Dialing	Rotary Phone
Beep, Tone	Directory Assistance	Teleconference
Call Forwarding	Information	Telephone Book
Call Waiting	International Operator	Three-Way Calling
Caller ID	Long Distance (Carrier)	Time & Charges
Calling Card	9-1-1	Toll-Free Number
Cellular Phone	Operator	Touch-Tone Phone
Collect Call	Pager	Voice Mail
		Yellow Pages

Faxes

Activity Report	Hook	Redial
Automatic Transmission	Jam	Remote Access
Broadcasting	Manual Dialing	Ring Volume
Control Panel Keys	Memory	Shift
Delayed Transmission	One-Touch Dialing	Signal
Function	Paper Jam	Speed Dial
		Super Quick Scan

E-Mail

Attachment	Lower Case Letters	Newsgroup
Bookmarks	Mailbox	Netiquette
Eudora®	In, Out	Netscape
Directory	R = Replied	Newsgroup
Domain	F = Forwarded	Online
E-Mail Address	Message is new/unread	Password
Home Page	D = Redirected the mail	Recipient
Hypertext (Hot) Links	Message	Timeout
Internet	Modem	World Wide Web

Acronyms

FAQ	Frequently Asked Questions
FTP	File Transfer Protocol
IP	Internet Protocol
IRC	Internet Relay Chat
URL	Uniform Resource Locators
WAIS	Wide Area Information Search
WWW	World Wide Web

Verbs

to attach (a document)	to delete	to save
to be (get) online	to download	to search
to connect	to empty (trash)	to surf
	to receive	

"Netiquette" is good manners on the Internet. Here are a few of the most common manners to remember:

1)   Don't flame. To flame means to call someone rude names and/or overly criticize an article.

2)   Don't spam. To spam means to send inappropriate articles or topics to many, most, or all newsgroups. Make sure your articles are appropriate to the group. Commercial postings should be sent only to commercial newsgroups.

3)   Don't YELL. Writing in capital letters signifies that you are yelling or speaking in an angry tone. Avoid writing in all capital letters.

After studying the meaning of the vocabulary words on the previous two pages, complete the following exercises to help you remember them longer.

1) Match the different functions on the right with the underlined numbers on the left.

_____	<u>4</u>-1-1	A. Fire, Police, Emergency
_____	1-800-555-1212	B. Collect Call, Operator Assisted, Calling Card Call
_____	<u>9</u>-1-1	C. Directory Assistance
_____	1-<u>801</u>-488-4255	D. Country Code
_____	011-<u>81</u>-3-3269-9632	E. Directory Assistance (for Toll Free Numbers)
_____	<u>011</u>-33-1-654-3210	F. Area Code
_____	<u>0</u>-503-838-0000	G. International Direct Dial Code

2) Write the words described by the following definitions:

Person who assists callers to make telephone calls   _____

Fees charged by phone companies for phone use   _____

Phones which can be used anywhere   _____

Directory of businesses with addresses and phone #s   _____

System used to send out one fax to many numbers   _____

System used to get a fax when you are out of the office   _____

The person who receives your phone call, fax, or e-mail   _____

Good manners to be used on the Internet   _____

The device necessary to hook up to the Internet   _____

To hang up (fax machine)   _____

3) Describe the following terms:

Call Forwarding   _____

Jam   _____

E-Mail Address   _____

Conference Call   _____

One-Touch Dialing   _____

Mailbox   _____

Voice Mail   _____

Super Quick Scan   _____

Collect Call   _____

to print out	=	to print (or give out) information on paper
to be on the line	=	to be calling on the phone
to go through	=	to transmit; to be able to send
to hang up on (someone)	=	to cancel a call; to stop talking without saying goodbye
to surf the web	=	to use the Internet

1) Rewrite the sentences on the left using the most suitable new idioms.

a)   My laser printer won't give me that information. I wonder if it is out of paper.

_____

b)   Someone is calling for you.

_____

c)   I can't send this fax.   I wonder if the machine is broken.

_____

d)   My girlfriend stopped talking in the middle of my call. What did I say wrong?

_____

e)   He is using the Internet right now.

_____

2) Answer the following questions using an appropriate new idiom.

a)   Why haven't you sent that e-mail to our customers in Europe?
b)   Where is my copy of the report?
c)   How do you spend your free time in the evenings?
d)   What did you do when you got a call from the telemarketer?
e)   Could you get Mr. Smith on the phone for me?

3) Fill in the blanks below with one of the new idioms.

1)   Ms. Gonzales, your husband is _____. Do you want to take the call or shall I take a message?

2)   Unless you put in a new ink cartridge, the printer won't _____those letters you wrote.

3)   You spend entirely too much time_____ .
        If you don't get back to work _you are going to get fired!!

4)   I've tried calling our branch office in Buenos Aires four times. But since I don't speak Spanish, the secretary keeps _____.

5)   I don't know what I am doing wrong. These faxes just won't _____.

ALL ABOUT TELEPHONING

As you know, the telephone, fax machine, and Internet can be used in many ways to send or receive messages. This page will focus on telephones and faxes.

Direct Dialing

To make a local call within your free calling area, dial the number without an area code. To make a long distance phone call (outside your local area), you will need to dial a 1 plus the area code.

International calls can be dialed directly by dialing 011 + the country code + city code + the local phone number. For international collect calls or calling card calls dial 001+ country code + city code + the local phone number. Either an operator or automatic instructions will come on the line to tell you what to do.

Directory Assistance

You can get the telephone number for any person or company in the United States by dialing 4-1-1. An automated voice will ask, "What city?" followed by "What state?" and finally, "What listing?" You tell the name of the city, the name of the state, and the name pf the person or company you are trying to contact. A few moments later, an operator will speak to you and you will be given the phone number.

Please remember that there is a charge of $.50 to $1.00 for each call you make for Directory Assistance, although in some areas you may ask for two numbers at one time at no additional cost.

When you dial Directory Assistance, you will be asked "What city?" After saying the name of the city, you will be asked, "What listing?" This means what is the name of the person or company you want to call. A few moments later, you will be given the number.

Calling Collect

Collect calls in the United States can be made by dialing 0 + Area Code + the local number. In many places the entire system is automatic. You state your name and the machine will ask the party you are calling if they will accept your call. If they say yes, you can speak. If they say no, you will not be able to talk to them.

Credit/Calling Card Calls

Dial 0 + the area code. Key in your card number and PIN (Personal Identification Number) after you hear the tone. Note: If you are using a rotary phone, you must wait until the operator answers the phone.

Toll-Free Calls vs. 900 Numbers

In the United States all toll free calls are identified by either 1-800 or 1-888. If you know the name of a company but do not know if they have a toll free number, you can dial 1-800-555-1212 to get the number. Toll free calls are free from public telephones too.

If you see a 1-900 number, there is always a cost (and usually a very high one!) for calls to these numbers. Don't confuse toll-free numbers with 900 numbers.

Emergency Calls

If you ever need to speak immediately to the police, the fire department, or an ambulance service, dial 911. When the operator answers, tell her quickly what the problem is and where you are or what your address is. 911 calls are always free, even from public telephones.

1)   If the phone number for your company in Seoul, Korea is (02)* 358-8922, what would the complete phone number be if you wanted to dial them directly from the U.S.?

2)   How much does directory assistance cost in your area?

3)   When might it be necessary to make a collect call?

4)   Is it better to make a collect call or use your calling card when dialing?

       a)   a family member
       b)   a business contact
       c)   your best friend

5)   When would it be appropriate to dial 911?

       a)   you cut off your finger and are bleeding badly
       b)   your boss has a heart attack after looking at your travel expenses
       c)   there's a small fire in a trash can in your office
       d)   the toilet in your office is overflowing and flooding the bathroom
       e)   you receive an obscene telephone call

6)   Write down an appropriate message for your office telephone answering machine.

7)   What kind of information should always be included in a fax if you hope for an answer?

8)   What is your e-mail address or what e-mail address would you like to have?

9)   What should offices which have access to the Internet do to prevent people from wasting work time (ie. playing games) on the Internet or using it to view inappropriate material?

*When making international calls, you do not need to use the "0." In this case, dial only "2."

Pair up with a partner and practice telephoning business contacts in the following situations:

1)   CALLING SOMEONE WHO IS THERE TO TAKE THE CALL

A: Hello. Sunshine Trading Company.

B: Hello. This is Mr. MacKay at Rockford Mineral Company. May I speak to Mr. Takahashi please?

A: Yes. One moment please.

2)   CALLING SOMEONE WHO IS NOT THERE TO TAKE THE CALL

A: Hello. President Shipping Lines.

B: Hi. This is Mr. Woodbury of the Bonita Banana Company. May I speak to Mr. Gomez?

A: I'm sorry. He isn't in right now. Would you like to leave a message on his voice mail?

B: Yes.

or

A: May I take a message?

B: Yes, please have him call me when he gets in.

A: Certainly. May I have your number, Mr. Woodbury?

B: It's area code 503-818-1234.

A: Let me repeat that. 5-0-3-8-1-8-1-2-3-4?

B: That's right.

A: Fine. I'll give Mr. Gomez your message.

3)   OTHER BUSINESS SITUATIONS

A: Mid-East Airlines.

B: Hello. I'd like to speak with Mr. Al-Dabbi.

A: I'm sorry. Mr. Al-Dabbi is:

           not at his desk (or away from his desk) at the moment.

           out of town on a business trip.

           away today.

           on vacation.

           in conference right now.

           with a customer right now.

           on another line.

B: When will he be back (or available)?

A: He should be back (or available) (day or time). Would you like to leave a voice mail message?

B: Yes, please.

       or   No, thank you. I'll call back.

4)   DIALING A WRONG NUMBER

A: Hello. Is this Staplers Office Products?

B: No. It isn't. You must have the wrong number.

A: I'm sorry. Is this 261-2722?

B: No, this is not 261-5722. or Yes, it is 261-2722, but this is not Staplers.

A: Sorry to have bothered you.

       or   I'm sorry. I'll check the number again.

TELEPHONE ETIQUETTE

1)   If you are a caller, do not say "hello" until your party has said "hello" first. Give the person time to pick up the phone.

2)   Introduce yourself on the phone as Mr. (Mrs./ Ms./ Miss) (plus your last name) or give both names without using Mr., Ms., etc.

       Ex.   This is Mr. Tanaka.   or   This is Kenji Tanaka.

3)   Because foreign names are sometime difficult to hear or to spell, spell your name after giving it. For example, "My last name is Fuentes. F-U-E-N-T-E-S." It is not usually necessary to give your first name.

4)   Americans do not usually make assuring comments like "Yes" or "I see" while the speaker is speaking. There is no problem if the listener makes such comments, but if you hear no comments from the other party, there is no need to say "hello" again and again.

5)   Always ask permission to use someone else's phone.

6)   Don't speak too loudly on the phone.

7)   If you reach a wrong number, apologize before hanging up.

8)   If possible, use a calling card, credit card, or phone card when using another person's phone for long distance calls. If calling direct, offer to pay for the call.

9)   Avoid making calls after 10:00 PM unless you are sure the person you are calling (or their family) will not be disturbed.

10)   Always say goodbye before hanging up.

ROLE PLAY

Teacher: Choose two students to practice calling each other in front of the other students in the class. One student should break as many rules as possible. Each time a rule is broken, the other students should indicate which one it was. This may also be used as a paired activity for all students at one time.

THE YELLOW PAGES

AUTOMOBILE DEALERS
Friendly Fred's Used Cars	2123 Henry Ford Dr.	756-9843
Lady Bug Volkswagen	3939 Allemand Rd.	254-4802

BAKERIES
Bud's Bakery & Pie Shop	747 Weight Watcher's Lp.	456-7890
Rosie's Pastry Shop	777 Sweettooth Ave.	357-6357

EMERGENCY SERVICES
Fire Department	898 Arson Hts.	255-1111 or 911
Police Department	1776 Uncle Sam Cir.	255-1100 or 911

ENGLISH COMPANIES
English-Is-Us	20 Grammar St.	234-4025
ESL School	1999 TOEFL Blvd.	345-6789

MORTUARIES
Morty's Mortuary	1313 Paradise Pl.	444-4444

MOVIE THEATERS
Mammoth Multiplex	378 Mammoth Blvd.	1-800-423-6981
Riverside Drive In	1200 Makeout Ln.	838-1234

RESTAURANTS
Big Mike's Drive In	1007 Heartburn St.	838-4865
Tang's Teriyaki	1028 Lampkin Ln.	654-9876

ASSIGNMENTS & ROLE PLAY

1)   Try to figure out the abbreviations used on this page (ex. Ln., St., etc.).

2)   Pair up with a partner and role play at least 3 of the tasks below:
   - a)   Call up a car dealer to find information on a new or used car.
   - b)   Call the mortuary to arrange a funeral for someone who has died.
   - c)   Call up a movie theater and find out what's playing, what times the movies start, what they are rated, and what the price of a ticket is.
   - d)   Call up the police or fire department to report a robbery or a fire.
   - e)   Call up an English school and ask for more information about their programs, costs, etc.
   - f)   Call up a restaurant and find out what's on special tonight, what their specialty dishes are, what their price range is, etc.
   - g)   Order a decorated birthday cake from the bakery.

BUSINESS LOGOS

Below you will find the logos for a variety of companies. Underneath each logo write the kind of company you think the logo represents. After completing the assignment, be prepared to explain why you labeled each logo the way you did.

_____ _____ _____ _____ _____

    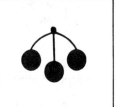

_____ _____ _____ _____ _____

  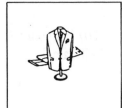  

_____ _____ _____ _____ _____

_____ _____ _____ _____ _____

1)   *If available in your area, call pre-recorded messages and write down the information you hear from the following:*

      a)   Movie theaters to hear what's playing, ratings, times, prices, etc.

      b)   Retail stores to hear store hours.

      c)   Weather service recordings to listen for temperature and forecasts.

      d)   Sports arenas to learn of upcoming sports events.

2)   *Choose one of the businesses categories listed below. Then, in the Yellow Pages, find three companies in that industry and call each of them to get the following information:*

a)	Car Rental Agencies	cheapest rates, mileage charges kinds of cars available, minimum age
b)	Hotels	Daily rates, discounts, check out times, special features
c)	Flower shops	Cost of 1 dozen roses; cost of delivery
d)	Pizza shop	Price of one large pepperoni pizza; cost of delivery

3)   *Design a full-page Yellow Pages advertisement for a business you would like to open. (See Business Plan Task #2 on Page 4.)*

MAILING & BUSINESS LETTERS
Letters & Packages

In the past, the types of services provided for mailing were relatively limited. Nowadays there are many things to keep in mind as a business person mails things. In this chapter, you will learn about business letter writing , mail services and other related issues.

VOCABULARY

#10 Envelope	Form Letter	S.A.S.E.
2nd-Day (Air)	Fragile	Salutation
Airmail	Letterhead	Signature
Box	Mailbox	Size Limits
Bulk Mailing	Package	Stamps
Certified Mail	Packing Material	Stationery
Direct Mail Marketing	Parcels	Weight Restrictions
Express Mail (Overnight)	Postage	Wrapping Paper
First Class	Postcard	
	Postmark	

1) Answer the following questions.

When would you enclose a self-addressed, stamped envelope (S.A..S.E.) in a letter you send?

You are advertising a special product that would only interest car salesmen.
What is one very effective way of getting the message of your product straight to them?

You are sending a letter that you want to make sure gets delivered directly to one particular person.
How would you send it?

What important information can you learn from the post mark?

What should you write on the outside of a package you are sending if there are breakable materials inside?
What symbols are used in your country to show that breakable materials are inside?

2) Fill in the blanks with an appropriate word from the vocabulary page.

_____ is what you would ask for if you wanted a package or a letter to be received quickly but not necessarily overnight.

There are _____ _____ and _____ _____ on parcels.

A _____ _____ would be the best thing to use if you have to send the exact same information to many different people.

Most forms and business letters require a _____ at the bottom of the page.

Make sure you put lots of _____ in this box before you send it. We don't want the things inside to move around toc much or break.

3) Many of the vocabulary words presented in this lesson can be divided into three different categories:
1) things you mail 2) mailing methods 3) things necessary to know or use to send mail.
Working with one or two others, place the new vocabulary words into the appropriate category.

Things to Mail	Mailing Methods	Things to know

to write down	=	to put something on paper
to put in black and white	=	to put important facts, information, or conditions on paper so nothing will be forgotten or lost
to read (look) over	=	to read or look at something from beginning to end rather quickly
to look forward to	=	to await joyfully; to anticipate eagerly

FREE RESPONSE: *Answer each question with an appropriate response.*

1) Please write down your name. _____

2) Please write down your phone number. _____

3) Write down your birthday, will you? _____

4) Can I get you to write down your hobbies? _____

5) Write down your teacher's good points. (Use as many pages as necessary.) _____

6) What kind of information needs to be put in black and white? _____

7) Why should all contracts be put in black and white? _____

8) What often happens when important information is not put in black and white? _____

9) What kind of information do some people NOT want to put in black and white? _____

FILL IN THE BLANK: *Fill in each blank with an appropriate word.*

1) Please read this _____ over before sending it to _____ .

2) Have the _____ read this over before faxing it.

3) There would have been fewer errors in this _____ if you had used your spell check before printing it.

4) Please look over this _____ before you sign it.

FREE COMPLETION: *Complete the following sentences with an original ending.*

1) I am looking forward to meeting her because. . .

2) Even though we were looking forward to his visit. . .

3) She doesn't look forward to Mondays at work because. . .

4) My family looks forward to payday because. . .

YOU TRY IT! *On a separate sheet of paper, make an original story using each of these new idioms.*

Below is one example of a standard business letter. In this example note how the main paragraphs are identified by both no indentation and a blank line between the paragraphs. Each part of the letter is labeled for easy identification. Page numbers tell you where to read more about that part of the letter.

A STANDARD BUSINESS LETTER

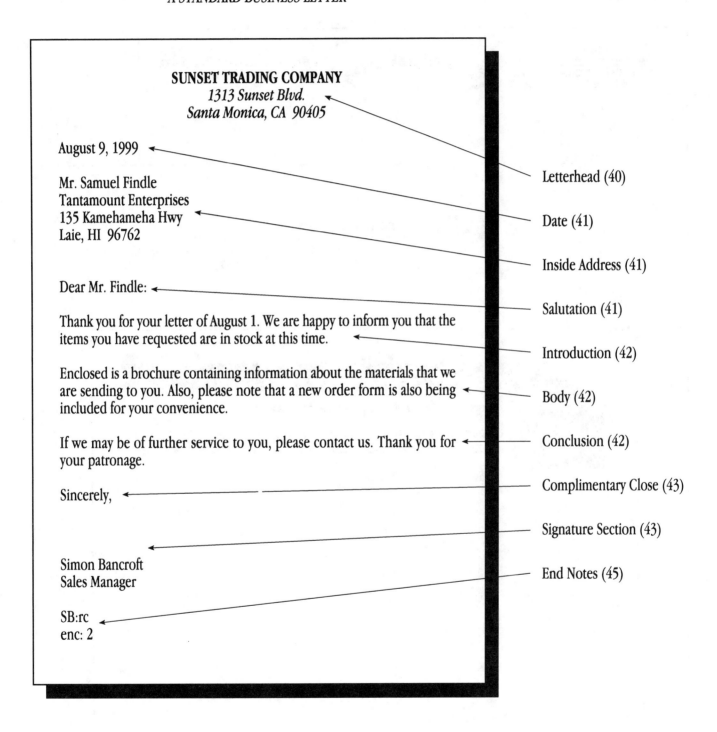

SUNSET TRADING COMPANY
1313 Sunset Blvd.
Santa Monica, CA 90405

August 9, 1999

Mr. Samuel Findle
Tantamount Enterprises
135 Kamehameha Hwy
Laie, HI 96762

Dear Mr. Findle:

Thank you for your letter of August 1. We are happy to inform you that the items you have requested are in stock at this time.

Enclosed is a brochure containing information about the materials that we are sending to you. Also, please note that a new order form is also being included for your convenience.

If we may be of further service to you, please contact us. Thank you for your patronage.

Sincerely,

Simon Bancroft
Sales Manager

SB:rc
enc: 2

Letterhead (40)

Date (41)

Inside Address (41)

Salutation (41)

Introduction (42)

Body (42)

Conclusion (42)

Complimentary Close (43)

Signature Section (43)

End Notes (45)

LETTERHEADS

The letterhead is a specially designed part of the business letter which is usually already printed on the stationery. The letterhead contains vital information about the company including the name, address, telephone number, fax number, and e-mail address. Sometimes the letterhead will use a logo or design which tells something about the company or the line of business.

SIGNATURE SIGN CO.
711 COLLEGE AVENUE
ALBANY, NY 12204

PHONE: (518) 454-4375
FAX: (518) 454-5204

KWIK FIX AUTO CENTERS

3000 North Studio Drive · Monticello, Indiana 46555
Phone: (219) 555-9375 · Fax: (219) 555-4273

NEW VISIONS EYE CLINIC

specializing in opthamology

777 NE Retina Drive • Vancouver, WA 91689
TEL (360) 555-7723 • FAX (360) 555-7724

Date

The first thing to place underneath your standard letterhead is the date the letter is being written. The date can be placed flush with either the right-hand or left-hand margin.

The Inside Address

Ordinarily, the inside address is placed along the left-hand margin one or two lines below the date. For the most part, it should closely resemble the address that will be typed on the envelope. Similar to the letterhead, the inside address also has a specified order to follow:

a) *the name of the person and/or title (title can go next to or under the person's name)*
b) *the name of his or her company*
c) *company address (street number and name)*
d) *city, state and zip code*

Even though including an inside address is standard protocol, there is a practical reason as well. Letters are often filed under the name of the company or person to whom they are sent. Writing this information at the top of your letters will make it easier to know where to file a copy of each one.

Notice of Attention

If you want to make sure that a certain person receives your letter, you can make a note of it by adding the word **Attention** two lines below the inside address. A colon (:) should separate the word Attention and the name of the person or the title of the person to receive the letter. Both name and title can be added if you know this information.

Examples: Attention: Ms. Nancy Stratton
                Attention: Personnel Manager
                Attention: Ms. Nancy Stratton, Personnel Manager

Salutation (Greeting)

The Salutation is typed two lines below the inside address or Attention notice. It too should be placed against the left-hand margin. A colon (:) is always placed after it in formal writing. Salutations will be different depending on the number of people you are writing to and whether or not you know their names.

For example, a greeting from column A could be used if you are writing to a business firm or a group of people in the firm rather than to any specific person. Salutations in column B would be used if you knew only the person's title. If you knew the actual name of the person to whom you are writing, the appropriate choice from column C would be most commonly used.

A	B	C
Gentlemen:	Dear Sir:	Dear Mr. (family name)*
Dear Sirs:	Dear Madam:	Dear Mrs. (family name)*
Ladies:	Dear Sir / Madam:	Dear Ms. (or family name)*
Dear Ladies:	Dear (position title)	

Special Advice
If you are writing to one specific person (especially if you are trying to develop possible sales contacts) take the time to make sure you're spelling the person's name correctly. See page 44 for other salutation suggestions.

The format of a business letter is made up of three main parts:

1) The Introduction   *2) The Message*   *3) The Closing*

The styles of business letter paragraphs are usually written in one of two ways: with the first line of each paragraph indented (left indent style) or with the first line against the left hand margin (block style). In either case, a space of two lines between each paragraph (including a space between the greeting and the introductory paragraph) is also common.

There are different reasons for sending business letters. Inquiries, sales prospecting, confirmation of information and many other purposes are common in business. The tone of a letter may change depending on your purpose for writing. As your purposes change, the content of your letters will naturally change also. However, the basic format (i.e., opening details, body, and closing details) should remain basically the same. In this section the format of a business letter will be explained.

The Introduction

After a simple greeting or a general statement of conditions (always make them positive), the first paragraph in your letter should clearly tell why you are writing the letter. If the letter is your first contact with the person or the business, you should use this introductory paragraph to briefly introduce yourself and your company and explain why you are writing. If you are writing in answer to a letter that you first received, you should indicate this. Below are a few examples of sentences found in these paragraphs:

> · Thank you very much for your letter dated January 12. In response to your question. . .
> · Let me be the first to take this opportunity to say how excited I am that. . .
> · After reading your brochure about insurance for my personnel I felt I still needed to ask. . .

The Body

After your introduction has explained to the reader why you are writing your letter, you should give further details concerning your purpose(s) in the main body of the letter. For the most part, the main body of a business letter simply is the place to explain in detail whatever was introduced in the introductory paragraph(s). The number of paragraphs needed in the body of your letter will, of course, vary depending on the number of topics you bring up or the complexity of the matters at hand.

The Conclusion

The final paragraph(s) of a business letter should be used to briefly review the most important points made in the main body of the letter and to provide a "closure" of that information. For example, if your purpose is to sell something, you should remind the reader how he or she can order your product. If you wrote to ask about something, make sure the reader knows where to send the answer(s) to your question(s).

It is also important in your final paragraphs to thank the reader for taking the time to read your letter and for the time and attention that will be spent in taking care of whatever actions are required. If you expect any action from the reader, you should politely remind him or her of this. Below are a few example sentences commonly found in conclusion paragraphs.

> · In conclusion, let me say thank you one more time for your attention to this matter. It will.....
> · I hope you will agree that in the future it will be mutually beneficial to meet and discuss......

After the body of a business letter, you will find the following: the complimentary close, a signature section, and any final secretarial notations. These will be discussed separately.

The Complimentary Close

A complimentary close is a one-, two-, or three-word phrase that politely says "good-bye" to your reader. It, too, is placed two lines below the paragraph above and most commonly "flushed left." However, it can be located in the center right region of the letter also. When more than one word is used in the complimentary close, only the first word is capitalized. The close is always followed with a comma (,). For example:

   Sincerely yours,   *or*   Most respectfully,

As the chart on page 44 demonstrates, there are many different complimentary closes. Usually the close that you use will depends on the salutation that was chosen to open the letter. Use the chart on page 44 to match the complimentary close with the salutation you choose.

The Signature Section

After the complimentary close, a few empty lines must be put in to allow space for your (or your boss's) signature. The number of empty lines to put in the letter will depend on the size of the signature to be signed. Generally, four lines are left between the complimentary close and the signature section. The signature section will first include the signature of the person who wrote or dictated the letter. Below the signature space the name of the sender should be typed out. Immediately after the typed name of the sender, the sender's job title and company can be added. Study the complimentary closes and signature sections provided below.

A) All business letters should be signed by hand. The signature should be in pen, not pencil. Since many signatures are illegible, it is important to type the name below the signature.

   EXAMPLE: Yours faithfully,

          Frank Spector

B) This typewritten repetition of the writer's name may be accompanied by his or her official position.

   EXAMPLE: Truly yours,

          James Kingley
          Managing Director

C) Sometimes you will see the name of the company typed just below the complimentary close or under the position or title of the person.

   EXAMPLE: Yours truly,   Yours truly,
          PROFITS LIMITED

                           Hank Ford
          Hank Ford   Financial Manager
          Financial Manager   PROFITS LIMITED

Use the chart below to match an appropriate salutation with a suitable complimentary close. Try to use variety in your letters rather than using the same salutations and closes each time.

COMPLIMENTARY CLOSE / SALUTATION ▶	Gentlemen:	Dear sirs:	Sirs:	Dear ladies:	Ladies:	Dear sir:	Dear madam:	Dear Mr. (family name):	Dear Mrs. (family name):	Dear Ms. (family name):	Dear Doctor (family name):	Dear Governor (family name):	Dear Professor (family name):	Dear Senator (family name):	Dear (first name):
Very respectfully yours,											■	■	■	■	
Yours very respectfully,											■	■	■	■	
Respectfully yours,											■	■	■	■	
Yours respectfully,											■	■	■	■	
Very truly yours,	■			■	■			■	■	■	■				
Yours very truly,	■			■	■			■	■	■	■				
Truly yours,	■	■	■	■	■	■	■	■	■	■	■				
Yours truly,	■	■	■	■	■	■	■	■	■	■	■				
Very sincerely yours,								■	■	■					■
Yours very sincerely,								■	■	■					■
Sincerely yours,								■	■	■					■
Yours sincerely,								■	■	■					■
Sincerely,								■	■	■					■
Very cordially yours,															■
Yours very cordially,															■
Cordially yours,															■
Yours cordially,															■
Cordially,															■
Faithfully yours,															■
Yours faithfully,															■

End Notations

The notations section is always the last thing to appear on a business letter. Essentially, three pieces of information are included in this section. Each notation is designed to give more information to the reader.

The Initials Line

Often, two people are involved in the writing of a business letter: 1) the sender and 2) his or her assistant. This is shown on the initials line. In the initials notation, the initials of the sender are typed in capital letters, followed by a slash(/) or a colon (:) followed by the initials of the person who actually typed the letter. The typist's initials are in lower-case letters.

> EXAMPLE: JK:sh

In the above example, the sender of the letter might be Jane Kiplinger (or any other person whose initials are J.K.) while the person who actually typed the letter might be Sharon Hopkins (or again, any person whose initials are S.H.).

Enclosures

In many business letters, extra information (pamphlets, flyers, etc.) is included in the envelope of the letter. So that the receiver of the letter does not overlook or accidentally throw away this added information, an Enclosure notation is added.

If there is just one enclosure, the most common practice is to simply type the word enclosure in the appropriate location. If there are two or more items, the word *enclosure* is abbreviated (encl.) followed by a colon(:) and the number of extra items in the envelope.

> EXAMPLE: encl: 3

In the above example, a receiver can expect to find three pieces of added material in the envelope.

CC:

This notation, followed by people's names, means that a copy of the letter is being sent to other people also. The letters "cc" stand for carbon copy. Even though copies of letters are now made with copy machines instead, the notation is still used.

> EXAMPLE: cc: John Buehner
>   Stacy Lyon

1) What is a practical reason for placing an inside address on a business letter?

2) How many lines should there be between the inside address and the salutation?

3) When addressing a person by name what is one of the most important things you should do?

4) How many lines should there be between the greeting and the first paragraph?

5) What style of business letter does not use paragraph indentation?

6) Name the three parts of a business letter's main text.

7) What is the purpose of a complimentary close?

8) What three items can commonly be found after the signature space of a business letter?

9) If the end note JR/ap is found at the bottom of the letter, what would that mean?

10) How many enclosures are in an envelope if only the word "Enclosure" is written at the bottom?

ALL ABOUT ENVELOPES

1)   This is the sender's name, address, and zip code. Some businesses include their telephone and fax numbers in this area as well. It is very important to fill in this area as letters sometimes do not reach their destinations and have to be returned. If there is no return address, the letters often end up in the "dead letter" file at the post office.

2)   This is where the stamp is placed. The only rule to remember is to place enough postage so that it does not come back or that the receiver does not have to pay "postage due" fees.

3)   This is the addressee's information. Notice that it is not written in the middle of the envelope, but rather in the bottom right-hand section. The information needed is as follows:

    a)   name
    b)   number and street name (apartment or suite number)
    c)   city, state, zip (postal) code
    d)   country

Find the mistakes in the letter below and explain why they are wrong.

February 23, 1999

Eastern Manufacturing Co.
31 International Square
New York, N.Y. 09915
U.S.A.

Godzilla Toy Company
16 Honshiocho
Minato-Ku, Tokyo
Japan 101

Attention: General Manager, Toshio Shimura

Gentlemen:

Thank you for your inquiry. We are very happy to inform you that we will be able to give you a 10% discount for shipments of our plastic components.

We are also pleased to tell you that your order of mini batteries was sent last week. You should be receiving them within a month.

We have enclosed three order forms for your convenience.

Thank you for giving us the opportunity to serve you and your company. We look forward to hearing from you.

Yours;

Export Manager
George M. Callahan

jc/FLS
Encl: 2

1)   Choose a company in your area and write a well-organized business letter to a person in that company asking for information regarding their products or services. In your letter make sure to ask for information regarding the following things:

        a) Brief company history
        b) What products / services they offer
        c) Prices
        d) Availability

2)   Choose any piece of mail from your mailbox. Identify these parts of the letter:

        a) Inside address
        b) Salutation
        c) Main text
        d) Complimentary closing
        e) Sender's title

3)   Create a letterhead and envelope design you would like to use for your new business. (See task #8 on Pg. 10)

SECTION 4

Business English Basics

BUSINESS BASICS
Companies, Workers & Competition

VIPS IN BUSINESS
businessman
businesswoman
customer
consumer
supplier
middleman
retailer
wholesaler

WHO'S WHO
CEO (chief executive officer)
president & vice president
management
salaried worker
owner
industrialist
entrepreneur

DEPARTMENTS & DIVISIONS
accounting (bookkeeping)
advertising
budget
merchandising
personnel
quality control
real estate
sales
cost control

GOVERNMENT
bureaucracy / red tape
regulations
GNP / SBA / IMF
balance of trade

LABOR UNION
workers
blue collar workers
white collar workers
salary / wages / pay
retirement benefits
raise
pension
insurance
hiring
firing
negotiations
contract

IN THE RED or BLACK
profit / loss
import / export
tariff
duty
shortage
surplus
dumping
inventory
pink slip

CORPORATIONS IN THE MIDST OF A BOOM
firm / company
headquarters
corporation
partnership
subsidiary
branch
stocks
stockholder
Wall Street

ROUGH COMPETITION
overhead / expenses
venture capital
interest rate
price war
credit
bid
policy / strategy / tactics
consumption
supply & demand

EQUIPMENT COSTS UP
appreciation
depreciation
expansion
modernization
computerization
automation
technology
mass production

1) What is the relationship between the following people?

 a) producer / wholesaler / retailer / customer (consumer)

 b) salaried workers / labor unions / management / stockholders

 c) customer / contractor / subcontractor / supplier

2) Describe the function of each person or organization listed below.

 a) labor union _____
 b) Madison Avenue _____
 c) board of directors _____
 d) middleman _____
 e) bureaucracy _____

3) Write a synonym for each of the following:

 a) tariff _____ f) supplier _____
 b) firm _____ g) accounting _____
 c) wages _____ h) headquarters _____
 d) overhead _____ i) customer _____
 e) bureaucracy _____

4) Write an antonym for each of the following:

 a) export _____ f) surplus _____
 b) profit _____ g) competition _____
 c) depreciation _____ h) purchase _____
 d) management _____ i) owner _____
 e) retailer _____

5) What does each of the following stand for?

 a) GNP _____ d) SBA _____
 b) H.Q. _____ e) Co. _____
 c) Corp. _____ f) Inc. _____

6) *Match the word on the left with its correct definition on the right:*

a) retailer	_____	a person who invests in the company by buying shares
b) real estate	_____	rules and laws that govern what a business can and cannot do
c) dumping	_____	land and buildings
d) negotiations	_____	the person who sells to the public
e) stockholder	_____	making things by machine to save human labor
f) overhead	_____	selling below cost to destroy competition
g) interest (rate)	_____	cost of doing business (rent, utilities, wages, etc.)
h) automation	_____	person who organizes and operates a business
i) regulations	_____	discussions to come to an agreement
j) entrepreneur	_____	cost of borrowing money from a lender

7) *Use the dictionary to find the meaning of the underlined parts of these words.*

a) auto<u>ma</u>tion, <u>auto</u>mation

b) <u>sal</u>ary

c) <u>sub</u>sidiary, sub<u>sidi</u>ary

d) manu<u>facture</u>, <u>manu</u>facture

e) <u>mono</u>poly, mono<u>poly</u>

f) bureau<u>cracy</u>, <u>bureau</u>cracy

g) techn<u>ology</u>, <u>techno</u>logy

h) computer<u>ization</u>

i) <u>president</u>, presi<u>dent</u>

j) <u>merchandising</u>

8) *From the list of words below, choose the most suitable word to fill in the blanks of the following paragraph. Use each word only once.*

computerize	workers	raises	accounting
management	benefits	CEO	corporation
negotiate	fired	stockholders	labor union
retirement pay			

I was recently hired by a large _____ to work in their _____ department. Because the corporation is trying to _____ its accounts, a number of _____ will have to be _____ . This makes _____ happy because they will be able to give higher dividends to the _____ as profits increase. However, the _____ _____ is unhappy because the workers will be fired. If the workers are fired, the labor union wants more_____ such as bigger _____ and more _____ _____ for the remaining workers. The _____ said he will not _____ with the labor union.

to think (something) over	=	to consider (something)
to meet (someone) halfway	=	to compromise (with someone)
to be busy (+ v-ing)	=	to be in the middle of (doing something); to be occupied
to be out of the question	=	to be impossible; there is no way we can permit (this)

TELEPHONE CONVERSATION:
Replace the underlined parts of the following conversation with the new idioms from this lesson.

A: Hello. This is Mr. Richman of Ellison Enterprises. May I speak to Mr. Perry?

B: I'm sorry, he's <u>occupied</u> talking to his new secretary right now. May I help you? This is Bruce Hill, his partner.

A: Yes. Have you had time <u>to consider</u> our proposal to merge?

B: Yes, but I'm afraid the proposal is <u>impossible</u> at this time. Our Board of Directors has turned down our request.

A: Aren't they willing <u>to compromise with us?</u>

B: I'm afraid not. They're the big shots* with all the say so** around here.

        (* big shot = bosses, management, CEOs   ** say so = right to decide or make decisions)

Make a list in the spaces below of items that you would like to bring up in a negotiating session with your spouse, friend, boss, or a company you deal with often.

1) I'd like you to think over the following items:

_____

_____

_____

2) I would be willing to meet you halfway on the following points:

_____

_____

_____

3) The following items would be out of the question:

_____

_____

_____

4) Because I am busy doing the following, I will not be able to meet with you:

_____

_____

_____

THE FREE ENTERPRISE SYSTEM IN THE UNITED STATES

1   The American free enterprise system is based on three important concepts: *incentives, competition,* and *innovation.*

2   *Incentives* work around the idea that if you have a particular talent or a good idea, and if you're willing to sacrifice your time and money, you will be able to reap the rewards. Incentive is the key to getting people to work hard and/or risk their money on the possibility of future profits.

3   Needless to say, all people who own businesses would not put in the required time, expense, and effort to build a business unless there was the promise of possible rewards. Profits from a business are what allow the company to expand, to develop new products or services, and to hire new employees. For some people, just having the freedom to work for themselves is incentive enough to go into business.

4   Today, more Americans than ever are striking out on their own to become entrepreneurs, people who run their own businesses. Surprisingly enough, nearly 40% of all new jobs created each year in the United States are those in small, entrepreneurial firms which employ fewer than 20 people.

5   The question might be asked, "Where is the incentive to work for a large, established company?" In order to keep their most talented workers from going off on their own, many large corporations are now offering employees shares in the company's profits or company stock.

6   Incentive breeds *competition.* One of the main philosophies behind free enterprise is that the more choices there are, the more the customer will benefit. With many companies competing for the same customer, each business tries to better its rivals and come up with innovative ways to win the customer. Some compete on quality, some on price, others on service, and still others on image.

7   At times, the free enterprise system is manipulated by monopolies and governments in an effort to keep competition down. A prime example of this occurred in the early 1980's when the United States asked Japan to "voluntarily" limit the number of cars it exported to the United States. The U.S. hoped that such limits would reduce the risk of failure among American car manufacturers who were unable to compete one on one with the Japanese.

8   In order to foster competition in the United States, though, the government has moved to deregulate more and more businesses. This means that the government reduces its role to foster competition in certain industries. With deregulation comes an increase in competition which gives customers more for their money in most cases.

9   Since a lack of government rules can harm customers, the United States has established truth-in-advertising laws which prevent companies from lying about their products. Anti-trust laws also prevent competitors from setting prices which may be unfair to customers.

10 Competition makes the marketplace a powerful instrument for efficiency and for serving customers' needs.

11 The third pillar in the free-enterprise system is *innovation.* Innovation is the way new ideas, products, and techniques enter the marketplace. Without people who invent and develop new ways to do things, the free-enterprise system would grind to a halt. And it is becoming more and more apparent in our high-tech economy that companies which do not innovate can't compete.

12 How does innovation spur the economy? For one thing, a successful innovation spawns even more innovations. It also makes things less costly and available to more people. Henry Ford's assembly line is a perfect example of how a costly product, the automobile, was made cheaper and thus more affordable to the general public by an innovation which became part of our history.

13 Whereas most innovations were produced by individual inventors in the last century (Goodrich, Edison, Bell, etc.), most innovations today are created by teams of scientists and engineers working together in government, industry, and in university labs. Large corporations, which were unable to compete with the innovative spirit of smaller companies, now work closely with universities to develop new ideas or group their own employees into small work teams to come up with potentially profitable innovations. Other companies offer big bonuses to their employees who come up with new ideas.

14 Innovation is a major force providing the United States with limitless potential for future growth.

In your business readings you will often come across words or phrases which are new to you. If you are in a hurry you may not have enough time to look up every new word. In such cases it is important to learn how to guess. The following list of words and phrases is taken from this reading. Tell what part of speech each is; then write a definition taken from the sentence context. Your teacher will give the actual definition for comparison. The number in parenthesis is the paragraph in which the word is found.

WORD	PART OF SPEECH	GUESSED DEFINITION	ACTUAL DEFINITION
sacrifice (2)			
reap (2)			
striking out (4)			
entrepreneurs (4)			
on their own (5)			
to better (6)			
manipulated (7)			
one on one (7)			
deregulate (8)			
foster (8)			
truth-in-advertising (9)			
grind to a halt (11)			
spur (12)			
spawns (12)			

Without referring to the reading pages, answer the following questions. Check your answers by rereading the paragraph in the number in parenthesis after completing the test.

1) What are the three pillars of the free enterprise system? (1)

2) Which one is the key to getting people to risk their money, time, and effort on the possibility of future rewards? (2)

3) Other than for profits, what is another major reason people try to establish their own businesses? (3)

4) What percentage of all new jobs created in the U.S. each year are found in small businesses? (4)

5) What are the four main ways in which businesses try to compete with each other? (6)

6) What is the main benefit of deregulation? (8)

7) What do truth-in-advertising laws try to prevent? (9)

8) What is the purpose of an anti-trust law? (9)

9) How did the assembly line make Henry Ford more successful? (12)

l0) How do big companies try to get their employees to come up with new ideas? (13)

SIZING UP THE COMPETITION

One of the basic principles of being effective in doing business is to know who your competitors are and what they are doing to compete with you. Here are some helpful hints on how to find what your competitors are doing.

1) Request to be put on your competitor's mailing list or call for the latest information. Most companies willingly send general information to anyone who asks.

2) Buy your competitor's products or services. By so doing, you can often find ways to improve your product and/or services and to outdo your competitor.

3) Spend time in your competitor's territory. Visit the same bars, restaurants, spas, and golf courses. You will be surprised what you can learn "through the grapevine."

4) Read industry publications. For a modest price your company can get valuable information on new trends and news about your competitors like factory expansion, equipment upgrading, new products, and new patents.

5) Buy some of your competitor's stock. You'll receive prospectives, annual reports, and quarterly earnings reports no matter how few shares you hold.

6) Hire professional Market Researchers. Similar to the information you can gather from industry publications, a market research firm can help you find out about new work in research and development (R&D), new patents, new products, and profit and loss statements.

7) Protect your own secrets:

   a) You may need to have employees sign patent and secrecy agreements or no-compete contracts.

   b) Caution your own employees about dropping important facts outside the office.

   c) Don't explain secret procedures or allow tours of places where secret procedures take place. (Not even reporters, family members, or students should be allowed on such tours.)

   d) If an employee quits or retires, make sure you talk to that person about the importance of keeping company secrets and that you expect that person to remain loyal to your company.

DISCUSSION QUESTIONS

1) What does your company do to size up the competition?

2) What publications should all people in your business field subscribe to?

3) What are the advantages and disadvantages of hiring a market research company?

4) What are some ways your company protects its secrets?

5) Would you sign a no-compete contract?

PROVERBS FOR BUSINESS

Below are commonly used proverbs that are helpful to remember in business. Think of an equivalent proverb in your own language and translate it into English in the space beneath each proverb. Describe a situation in which you could have used one of these proverbs recently. Then tell which is your favorite proverb and why.

God helps those who help themselves.

Many hands make light work.

An egg today is better than a hen tomorrow.

The early bird catches the worm.

Don't count your chickens before they're hatched.

Strike while the iron is hot.

Waste not, want not.

You never get something for nothing.

A small leak may sink a big ship.

When the cat's away, the mice will play.

All work and no play makes Jack a dull boy.

All's well that ends well.

BUSINESS OCCUPATIONS
Business Jobs & Careers

VOCABULARY

HELP WANTED

Accountant needed at prestigious N.Y. company (Embezzlers Inc.) Call 555-2129 for an appointment.

Advertising Executive needed by major publisher. Write now to *Illiterates Illustrated.* 439 Write Brothers Drive, Reading, PA 19087.

Architect wanted now! Dynamic company urgently needs an experienced architect to work on project in Saudi Arabia. Call BechTel at 555-3322.

Bank-- Loan officer needed at Bank of USA. Experience necessary. Contact us by e-mail at *loans@bankusa.com.*

Business Men & Women Get rich quick! Call Pyramid Marketing Systems at 555-2311.

Cashier Elegant Scottish Pizza restaurant now hiring cashiers. References required. Call MacDominos at 555-1200.

CEO Chief Executive Officer needed at Boromoke Industries where our motto is: "Profits First, Safety Last." Fax resume to 555-9987.

Computer Program Specialist Sonny Corporation is looking for an experienced computer programmer willing to relocate to Singapore. Call Mr. Mori at 555-5531.

Construction Workers White and Blue collar workers needed by *Titanic Shipyards*. Send resume to TSY, NY Harbor, NY 10011

HELP WANTED

Dentist Small Pennsylvania town urgently needs more dentists. Call collect: 555-35-SMILE. in Hershey, PA.

Environmentalist We are a new environmental lobbying group. If you love trees and if you have experience in either lobbying or environmental studies, call us at 1-800-HUG-A-TREE.

Engineer wanted by first-rate manufacturing company. Call Edison Light Co. at 1-800-LITEN UP.

Entertainer Actors and actresses needed for upcoming sequel to famous movie. Ask for the director of *"Gone Out the Window"* at 555-3434.

Executive Secretary to Fortune 500 CEO. Send resume to Walton Brothers Co. Fayetteville, AR.

General Manager needed by real estate firm to head new branch in booming area of North Dakota. Contact Swen Swenson at PO Box 9989543, Forgo, N.D. 58689.

Factory Workers We need you now! Call 555-8983.Top pay. Great Benefits. American Steel Co. Cleveland, Ohio.

Market Forecaster needed by Herbert Hoover Investment Co. "We Know Our Stuff." 611 Wall St. NY, NY 10010.

Truck Driver U-Maul Movers is looking for career long-distance moving van drivers. No experience necessary. Will train. Call 1-888-UMAUL today.

SITUATION WANTED

Chairman of Stock Brokerage desires new challenges. Write: 321 NE Ell, Aloha, OR 97111

Designer Homes, offices, etc. I design anything. Reasonable prices. Frank Rite. 555-3499.

Entrepreneur Worked for major fruit-related computer manufacturer for 23 years. Call 555-0021. Ask for Steve.

Looking for a **Financier** with money to invest. Call Bermuda Laundry Company where our motto is *"We'll take you to the cleaners."* See our ad in the Yellow Pages under *Cleaners.*

Mechanic with lots of experience. Call Joe Goodwrench at 313-FIXACAR.

Lawyer Once worked for U.S. President. Lots of contacts. Write Arizona State Prison, Cell 717, Tuscon, AZ 87564

Sales Representative for American car company in Tokyo, Japan. Will not work on commission. Write PO Box 999, this newspaper.

Personnel Manager for large sports shoe company. Ask for Mikee at Nikee. 555-6723

Unemployed for years. I need and want a job badly. Former used car salesman. Call the downtown Mission and ask for "Slick Mick." 555-4000

1) *Look up one or two verbs to match each occupation on the Vocabulary Page.*
Write a sentence using the new verbs and vocabulary words.

Example:	loan	The banker said they can't loan me money because I have no job.
	invest	The banker said they would be happy to invest my money for me.

2) *List the occupations on the previous page which have the following endings:*

man (woman)	er/or	-ian	-ist	-ier/yer

3) *Look up the roots of the following words in the dictionary. The words in parenthesis also come from the same roots. What languages do these words come from?*

a) politician (police, metropolitan)   e) supervisor (superior/vision)

b) manufacture (manicure; manipulate)   f) secretary (secrecy)

c) architect (arch-enemy)   g) construction (consider; structure)

d) president (prescribe; reside)   h) forecaster (forehead)

4) *Where do the following people work or perform their duties?*

a) secretary   d) entertainer   h) accountant

b) dentist   e) designer   i) CEO

c) lawyer   f) mechanic   j) architect

g) cashier

thanks to (someone/something)	=	owing to; because of
A.S.A.P.	=	as soon as possible; immediately
to do (one's) best	=	to try as hard as possible
to count on (someone, something)	=	to depend on (someone/thing); to trust

STORY TRANSFORMATION: *Rewrite the story below using the new idioms in the underlined parts.*

In our company we are looking for a new (choose an occupation). In order to find someone <u>immediately</u> we need to advertise in many places. <u>Because of</u> modern computers we can match that person's qualifications with the job. We want someone we can <u>trust</u>. We need someone who will <u>try as hard as possible</u> to help our company grow. Do you have any recommendations?

TRUE / FALSE: *After answering true or false, tell why it is true or false or give an example.*

    1) Your boss / teacher always wants you to do things A.S.A.P. Why?

    2) _____ is a person you can always (never) count on.

    3) Even if you don't do your best you will not be fired.

    4) Thanks to your teacher you are learning excellent English. (No choice!)

FREE RESPONSE: *Answer each question appropriately.*

    1) What is the difference between A.S.A.P. and "at your convenience?"

    2) When do you always try to do your best? When do you rarely do your best?

    3) What happens to people who can't be counted on at all times?

    4) What (product, knowledge, information, etc.) do you have thanks to (TV, education, the Internet, etc.)?

YOU TRY IT! *On a separate sheet of paper, make an original story or sentences using each of the new idioms.*

WHAT'S YOUR OCCUPATION?
(At a party, two business people are introduced to each other)

Hopkins: How do you do? My name is Marsha Hopkins.
(They shake hands)

LeBlanc: Nice to meet you. I'm Francois LeBlanc.

Hopkins: Where are you from, Mr. LeBlanc?

LeBlanc: Please call me Francois. I'm from France.

Hopkins: Oh? Where in France?

LeBlanc: I'm from Marseille in Southern France.

Hopkins: I see. What's your occupation?

LeBlanc: I'm a sales representative. Let me give you my card.
(They exchange business cards.)

Hopkins: Thank you. *(She looks carefully at the card)* Who are you with?

LeBlanc: I'm with the F.B.I.

Hopkins: You're kidding! The American F.B.I.?

LeBlanc: No, the French F.B.I. It stands for French Bonbon Industries. We make candy.

Hopkins: Sounds interesting. How long have you been with F.B.I.?

LeBlanc: I've been with them for 10 years. Now, please tell me about yourself, Marsha.
(Conversation continues. . .)

SEXISM

Since the advent of the woman's liberation (feminist) movement in the late 1960's, many changes have taken place in the way names are given to certain occupations in the business world. Names which give the feeling that only one sex is able to do that job are gradually being replaced with nonsexist names. Many people hope that this will help rid American society of sexism, generally considered a bias against women. Of course, a job title must describe what a person doing that job does. Let's take a look at some sexist titles and their safe equivalents below.

SEXIST	**SAFE**
airline steward(ess)	flight attendant
fireman	firefighter
foreman	supervisor
watchman	guard
newspaperman	news reporter
policeman	police officer
saleslady (salesman)	clerk

COFFEE OR TEA?

POINTS FOR DISCUSSION:

1) What other occupations can you think of that suggest only a man or woman can do that job?

2) What would be a safe title for a maid, paperboy, mailman, etc.?

3) What barriers do women face in your country in finding work, receiving equal pay, and progressing "up the ladder"?

4) What jobs do you feel women or men are unsuited for? Why?

DILEMMA

As a personnel manager of a mid-sized U.S. engineering company, you have just interviewed two excellent candidates for employment in your Mideast representative office in Egypt. One candidate is a woman graduate of Harvard University in engineering. She speaks almost fluent Arabic. The other candidate is a male graduate of Stanford University in engineering with no foreign language background. Whom would you choose? Why?

DISCRIMINATION

To avoid charges of prejudice against people because of race, age, sex, and the like, American employers have to be very careful about questions they ask during a pre-employment interview or on a job application. Below are some of the questions to avoid. Discuss why each item might be considered illegal and which ones might be asked *after* the person is hired.

1) Will you please send a picture of yourself with your application?

2) What race are you?

3) What sex are you? *(The only job where this question is legal is for a restroom attendant.)*

4) How old are you? *(This question can be asked is if there is a minimum age limit required by law.)*

5) Do you speak any foreign languages? *(Unless another language is necessary for the job.)*

6) What are your parent's names?

7) What clubs or organizations do you belong to?

8) What church do you attend?

9) What is your marital status?

10) How many children do you have? Who will take care of your children while you are at work?

11) When and where were you born?

12) What color are your eyes and hair?

13) What is your height and weight?

14) Do you have any physical disabilities? *(When can this question be asked?)*

15) What school did you go to?

SYMBOLS

Below are several symbols that can be used to represent various types of careers. See if you can tell which career field is represented by which symbol. Write the letter of the symbol on the line next to the corresponding career field listed at the bottom of the page.

1. ACCOUNTING   _____
2. ARBITRATION   _____
3. BANKING   _____
4. COMPUTER SCIENCE_____
5. ENGINEERING   _____
6. INVENTORY   _____

7. MANAGERIAL   _____
8. PERSONNEL   _____
9. POLITICS   _____
10. PUBLIC RELATIONS _____
11. SALES   _____
12. TEACHING

EMPLOYMENT APPLICATION

Based on the cultural discussion about discrimination, pair up with a partner and conduct an interview. The applicant should let the interviewer know which questions are irrelevant and which are not legal to ask.

THE BANDANA BANANA COMPANY

GENERAL INFORMATION

JOB TITLE: DATE OF BIRTH:

NAME: PLACE OF BIRTH:

ADDRESS: PHONE:

AGE: SEX:

MARITAL STATUS: SPOUSE'S NAME:

PARENTS' NAMES & ADDRESS:

NUMBER OF CHILDREN & AGES:

DO YOU OWN OR RENT YOUR HOUSE?

EDUCATIONAL BACKGROUND

HIGH SCHOOL / COLLEGE / TRADE SCHOOL	YEARS COMPLETED	COURSES

PHYSICAL INFORMATION

HEIGHT:	WEIGHT:	HAIR COLOR:	EYE COLOR:	RACE:

PLEASE LIST ANY PHYSICAL LIMITATIONS OR DISABILITIES WHICH MAY AFFECT YOUR JOB:

MISCELLANEOUS

WHERE ARE YOUR PARENTS FROM?

DO YOU SPEAK ANY FOREIGN LANGUAGES?   SPECIFY:

PLEASE LIST ANY REFERENCES WHICH WE MAY CONTACT:

ATTACH
RECENT
PHOTOGRAPH
HERE

SIGNATURE:

ASSIGNMENT

As part of this lesson and Business Task #9 (see Page 11), in the space below prepare an employment application form for your new business.

EMPLOYMENT APPLICATION FORM

ASSIGNMENTS

1)   Translate your company's motto into English.

2)   Read through the Help Wanted section of a local newspaper. Cut out and paste onto a separate sheet of paper information on five jobs that you would be qualified for and/or would be interested in applying for.

3)   Design an advertisement to place in a magazine or newspaper that advertises your company's products or services. Which publication would you place your ad in and why?

4)   Make a list of rules of etiquette which a person who visits your country should be aware of.

BUSINESS ORGANIZATION
Types of Companies

VOCABULARY

CORPORATE STRUCTURE

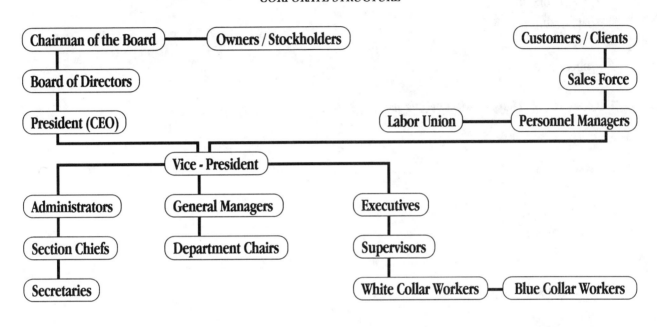

Chairman of the Board	—	Owners / Stockholders		Customers / Clients
Board of Directors				Sales Force
President (CEO)		Labor Union	—	Personnel Managers

Vice - President

Administrators	General Managers	Executives
Section Chiefs	Department Chairs	Supervisors
Secretaries		White Collar Workers — Blue Collar Workers

TYPES OF COMPANIES

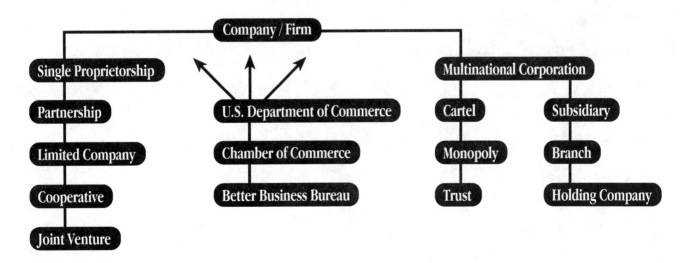

Company / Firm

Single Proprietorship		Multinational Corporation	
Partnership	U.S. Department of Commerce	Cartel	Subsidiary
Limited Company	Chamber of Commerce	Monopoly	Branch
Cooperative	Better Business Bureau	Trust	Holding Company
Joint Venture			

Choose one student to lead this discussion of vocabulary and vocabulary-related topics.

1)   **Find out the meaning of the underlined parts of each of the following words. Then list one or two more words which are derived from or contain that part.**

EXAMPLE: ad<u>ministr</u>ator = ministro = to serve   administration, minister, ministry, etc.

1. <u>bureau</u>crat
2. super<u>vis</u>or
3. <u>propr</u>ietorship
4. partner<u>ship</u>
5. con<u>tract</u>or
6. <u>sub</u>contractor

2)   **Who are they? (They) are the people who. . . ?**

1. owners
2. board of directors
3. customers (clients)
4. blue collar workers
5. secretaries
6. personnel

3)   **What do they do?**

1. union leaders
2. white collar workers
3. bureaucrats
4. department chairs
5. Chamber of Commerce

4)   **What kind of company is a. . . ?**

1. single proprietorship
2. joint venture
3. limited company
4. cartel
5. monopoly
6. subsidiary
7. cooperative

BUSINESS ORGANIZATION
Types of Companies

CORPORATE STRUCTURE

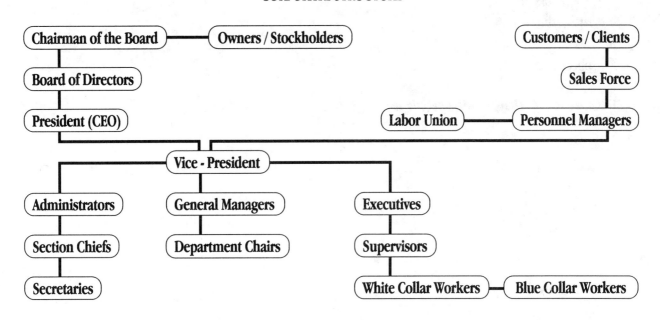

TYPES OF COMPANIES

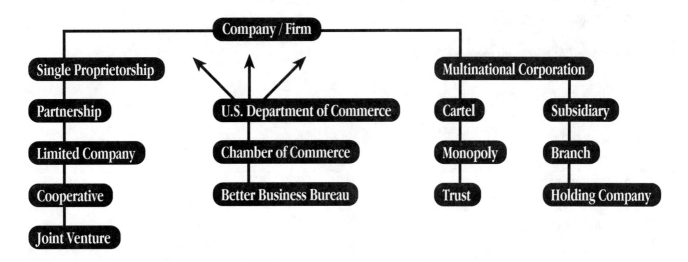

Choose one student to lead this discussion of vocabulary and vocabulary-related topics.

1)   ***Find out the meaning of the underlined parts of each of the following words.***
      Then list one or two more words which are derived from or contain that part.

        EXAMPLE: ad<u>ministr</u>ator = ministro = to serve   administration, minister, ministry, etc.

        1. <u>bureau</u>crat
        2. super<u>vis</u>or
        3. <u>propriet</u>orship
        4. partner<u>ship</u>
        5. con<u>tract</u>or
        6. <u>sub</u>contractor

2)   ***Who are they? (They) are the people who. . . ?***

        1. owners
        2. board of directors
        3. customers (clients)
        4. blue collar workers
        5. secretaries
        6. personnel

3)   ***What do they do?***

        1. union leaders
        2. white collar workers
        3. bureaucrats
        4. department chairs
        5. Chamber of Commerce

4)   ***What kind of company is a. . . ?***

        1. single proprietorship
        2. joint venture
        3. limited company
        4. cartel
        5. monopoly
        6. subsidiary
        7. cooperative

to step down	=	to retire or leave a position
to go through channels	=	to send a request or complaint through the correct chain of command
to take (something) up with (someone)	=	to consult with (someone) about (something)
to have a word with	=	to talk to (someone); to speak to
to be in charge of	=	to manage; to be responsible for

REWRITE: Rewrite the following sentences using the new idiom.

    a) No one knows who is responsible for the sales division in this company.

    b) A number of supervisors were forced to leave their positions after the strike.

    c) The Board of Directors asked to speak to the union officials.

    d) In order to make a request like that, you have to send it through the correct chain of command.

    e) The workers will have to consult with the company president about their pay raises.

FREE RESPONSE: Respond to the following sentences, using the correct idiom in your answers.

    a) Why did you have a word with your boss about your bonus?

    b) Who would you like to see step down in your company? Why?

    c) With whom do you take up your problems in your company? Why?

    d) Which channels do you go through to get a raise in pay or to make a complaint?

    e) What are you in charge of in your company?

FREE COMPLETION: Complete the following sentences:

    a) Our department chairman stepped down because. . .

    b) If you don't go through channels in our company. . .

    c) He was in charge of the accounting books until. . .

    d) Although he took up the matter with the Vice President. . .

    e) I'd like to have a word with those blue collar workers who. . .

YOU TRY IT! On a separate sheet of paper, use all five idioms in a business letter.

SAMPLE RESUME

Karyn Talbert
88 Olympia Street, Townhouse 31
Tifton, Georgia 31796
(912) 555-1998

CAREER OBJECTIVE
Position as director of corporate advertising in a Fortune 500 company.

PROFESSIONAL EMPLOYMENT

Company: Illiterates Illustrated
Duration: 11 / 95 - present
Position: Advertising Manager
Duties: Supervision of production and advertising for national magazine specializing
               in project management for public agencies.

Company: Sonny Corporation
Duration: 9 / 92 - 10 / 95
Position: Associate Advertising Director
Duties: Worked with the major advertising agencies to develop television and print ads
               for the U.S. Sonny Electronics Corporation.

Company: American Steel Company
Duration: 8 / 88 - 8 / 92
Position: Personnel Manager
Duties: Supervised an administrative budget and a staff of 35 full-time employees. In
               charge of screening and hiring new employees, employee evaluations, and
               putting together employee benefit packages.

EDUCATION

1984 - 1985	1977 - 1981
Central University, Rockford, IL	Madison College, Greattown, MA
Master of Arts in Advertising	Bachelor of Arts in Economics

ORGANIZATIONS

1994   City Council Member, Tifton, GA
1992   Board Member, Advertisers of America
1980   Student body President, Madison College

HONORS / PUBLICATIONS
Listed in "Who's Who in American Colleges"
Published article entitled "Are Your Ads a Minus?" in *Advertisers Weekly*.

REFERENCES
Available upon request.

YOUR OWN RESUME
Fill in the necessary information below to create your own resume.

NAME:
Address:

CAREER OBJECTIVE:

PROFESSIONAL EMPLOYMENT:
Company:
Duration:
Position:
Duties:

Company:
Duration:
Position:
Duties:

Company:
Duration:
Position:
Duties:

EDUCATION:

ORGANIZATIONS:

HONORS / PUBLICATIONS:

SPECIAL ABILITIES:

REFERENCES:

ADVERTISING SLOGANS

One of the most important points to remember in business advertising is how to catch people's attention. If you can come up with a slogan or phrase that stays in people's minds all day or write a tune that people remember and sing from time to time, you have created a successful marketing device. Take a look at the list of slogans below and match the slogan with the company you think created it from the column on the right.

1) "Mends everything but a broken heart"	_____	Greyhound Bus Company
2) "Always"	_____	McDonald's®
3) "Let your fingers do the walking"	_____	KFC®
4) "Family Car of the Air"	_____	Slumber Bed Company
5) "Babies are our business-our only business"	_____	Maxwell House Coffee
6) "Put a tiger in your tank"	_____	Clairol Hair Coloring
7) "The king of beers"	_____	The Kellogg Company
8) "Breakfast of Champions"	_____	Nike
9) "For the REST of your life"	_____	Fix-All Liquid Cement Company
10) "You deserve a break today"	_____	Coca-Cola
11) "Good to the last drop"	_____	Wheaties Cereal
12) "Does she...or doesn't she?"	_____	Gerber Baby Products Inc.
13) "Raise your hand if you're sure"	_____	Fisher-Price Toys
14) "How do you spell relief?"	_____	Visine Eye Drops
15) "Our work is child's play"	_____	Leslie Salt Company
16) "Finger Lickin' Good"	_____	Carnation Milk Company
17) "Profit First, Safety Last"	_____	AT&T Yellow Pages
18) "Gets the red out"	_____	Rolaids (stomach medicine)
19) "From contented cows"	_____	Cessna Aircraft Company
20) "Leave the driving to us"	_____	Exxon Gasoline
21) "The best to you each morning"	_____	Boromoke Industries
22) "When it rains, it pours"	_____	Budweiser
23) "I can"	_____	Sure Deodorant

Match the following slogan beginnings with their correct endings.

a) "Bring out the Best Foods,   without it." (American Express)

b) "If you think clothes don't make a difference, poor windows." (Anderson Windows)

c) "The more you eat,   the name goes on." (Sylvania TV)

d) "A woman never forgets   with Blue Bonnet on it." (margarine)

e) "Only the rich can afford   and bring out the best." (mayonnaise)

f) "Everything's better   forever." (jewelry)

g) "Profit first,   is Folgers in your cup." (Coffee)

h) "Quality goes in before   try walking down the street without any." (Tailor)

i) "Don't leave home   the more you want." (Cracker Jacks caramelcorn)

j) "A diamond is   Safety last." (Boromoke Industries)

k) "And away go troubles   the man who remembers." (Whitman's Chocolates)

l) "Nestles makes the very best   down the drain." (Roto-Rooter Drain cleaner)

m) "The best part of waking up   chocolate."

THE MULTINATIONAL COMPANY

As the world shrinks in size because of advances in transportation and communications, the number of multinational companies also increases. With this increase comes increased problems. The first one is how to handle relationships between overseas subsidiaries and the head office. The second one is how to handle problems between the subsidiary and the host government in the foreign countries where the subsidiaries are located.

When subsidiaries are first established they tend to have much autonomy, but as they become more important to the corporation the controls become tighter. Some companies then establish international divisions which are separated from the domestic divisions.

Many multinational companies put great emphasis on developing an elite group of managers who associate closely with managers of the company's other foreign subsidiaries. Together, these managers share operating experiences in different parts of the multinational company's "empire." Decisions are not made collectively but all managers accept common goals.

The problem is that occasionally these common goals may not be in the best interest of the host country. This often puts the local manager, usually a native of the host country, in a perplexing situation. Does loyalty come first to company or country?

QUESTIONS FOR DISCUSSION:

1) What would you do if...?

    ...the head office wanted to transfer a large amount of capital back to the headquarters at a time when the host country's currency is already very weak?

    ...the head office wants to reinvest most of the subsidiary's profits into the local facility but insists that all the equipment be bought in the country where the head office is located?

    ...the subsidiary is making high profits but political pressure in the country where the headquarters is located demands that the subsidiary be sold to locals or be closed?

    ...the goals established by the majority of the multinational managers are in cultural or political conflict with the host country where you are manager?

2) Comment on the following:

    a) What are some large multinational companies headquartered in your country?

    b) What advantages are there to working for a multinational company? Disadvantages?

    c) What are some common goals managers from the subsidiaries might make?

    d) What are some problems and areas of conflict that foreign-based multinational companies might have in your country?

ASSIGNMENTS

1) Write down and translate about ten well-known advertising slogans currently in use in your country.

2) Make a business organization chart for the company you work for or the school you attend.

3) Make a business organization chart for your proposed new business. (see task 9 on page 11)

4) List 5 duties for each person on the organization chart.

SECTION 5

English In The Workplace

THE OFFICE WORKER

VOCABULARY

SECRETARY VERBS:

to type   to file
to staple   to send (e-mail)
to answer (phones)   to screen (calls)
to write (letters)   to order (supplies)

OFFICE WORKER VERBS:

to work (overtime)   to be with a customer
to prepare   to be in charge of
to oversee   to head
to do busy work   to dress for success

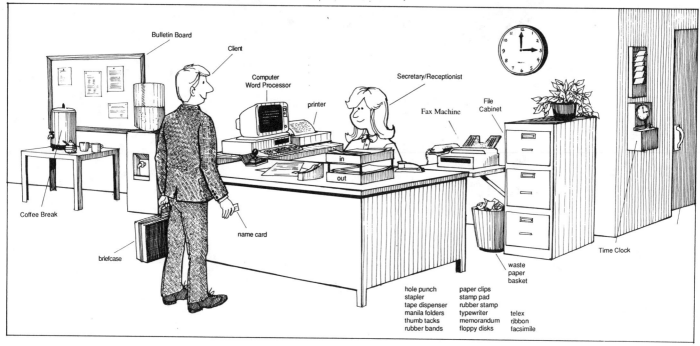

Bulletin Board
Client
Computer Word Processor
printer
Secretary/Receptionist
Fax Machine
File Cabinet
Coffee Break
in
out
name card
briefcase
Time Clock
waste paper basket

hole punch   paper clips
stapler   stamp pad
tape dispenser   rubber stamp
manila folders   typewriter   telex
thumb tacks   memorandum   ribbon
rubber bands   floppy disks   facsimile

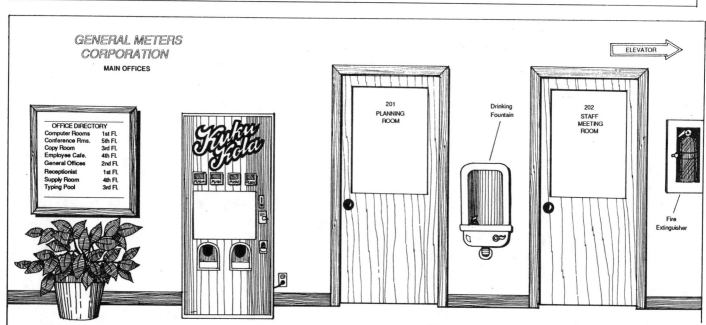

GENERAL METERS CORPORATION
MAIN OFFICES

ELEVATOR

OFFICE DIRECTORY
Computer Rooms   1st Fl.
Conference Rms.   5th Fl.
Copy Room   3rd Fl.
Employee Cafe.   4th Fl.
General Offices   2nd Fl.
Receptionist   1st Fl.
Supply Room   4th Fl.
Typing Pool   3rd Fl.

201
PLANNING
ROOM

Drinking
Fountain

202
STAFF
MEETING
ROOM

Fire
Extinguisher

Choose a student to lead the discussion of the vocabulary assignments.

1) Tell what each machine or item is used for.

Ex.   What is a copy machine used for? *It's used for making copies (reproductions).*

a) time clock
b) vending machine
c) elevator
d) word processor
e) stapler
f) paper clip
g) filing cabinet
h) thumb tack
i) rubber band
j) modem

2) Using "and things like that" (i.e., etc.), tell two or three things each of the following people do.

Ex.   A secretary types letters, answers phones, takes dictation, and *things like that.*

a) receptionist
b) employee
c) office worker
d) typist

3) Using the relative pronoun "where," tell what these rooms, places, or things are used for.

Ex. A file cabinet is a place *where* important papers, documents, and files are kept.

a) employee's cafeteria
b) waste basket
c) conference room
d) computer room
e) supply room
f) staff meeting room

4) General questions for discussion.

a) When is your starting time?   Your quitting time?
b) When do you punch in at the time clock?
c) When do you take your coffee break (your lunch hour)?
d) How often do you work overtime?

5) Teacher's Choice

to have a voice in (+ noun) / (+ v-ing)	=	to have some say or direction in
to be easy to work for	=	used to describe a superior whom you enjoy working with
to talk over (something)	=	to discuss with someone; to consult someone (about) someone
to call it a day	=	to quit for the day; to go home

FREE COMPLETION: *Complete the following sentences.*

1) A client can have a voice in product design if. . .

2) The receptionist doesn't have a voice in office policy because. . .

3) Although we'd like to have a voice in what's served at the employee's cafeteria. . .

4) The boss has a voice in everything since. . .

5) Make an original sentence using the idiom *to have a voice in*.

FREE RESPONSE: *Answer each question with an appropriate response.*

1) Why (is, isn't) your boss easy to work for?

2) Who do you think is the easiest person in your office to work for?

3) Why (or why not) would most people say you are easy to work for?

4) Describe the qualities of a person who is easy to work for.

5) Make an original sentence using the idiom *to be easy to work for*.

FILL IN THE BLANK: *Fill in the blank with an appropriate phrase.*

1) We held a conference so we could talk over the _____ .

2) During our coffee break we talk over _____ .

3) The supply room manager wants to talk over _____ with _____ .

4) She's in the planning room talking over _____ .

5) Make an original sentence using the idiom *to talk over*.

FREE RESPONSE & FREE COMPLETION

1) At what time do you usually call it a day?

2) I'm afraid we're going to have to call it a day because. . .

3) We called it a day at 4:30 in order to. . .

4) At what time would you like to call it a day everyday?

5) Make an original sentence using the idiom *to call it a day*.

A TOUR OF THE OFFICE

Guide: Good afternoon. Welcome to (name of company).
Before we begin, do you have any questions?

Visitor: Yes. What does your company do? (Or: What kind of company are you?)

Guide: We _____

Visitor: What are the major divisions or departments in this company?

Guide: _____

Visitor: What department do you work in?

Guide: _____

Visitor: What is your job? (What are you in charge of?)

Guide: _____

Visitor: How many people work for this company?

Guide: _____

Visitor: What percentage are white collar, blue collar; and what percentage
are full-time and part-time employees?

Guide: _____

Visitor: What benefits does this company offer its employees?

Guide: _____

Visitor: Where are your other major offices or branches?

Guide: _____

Visitor: Why did you choose to work at this company?

Guide: _____

Visitor: Thank you for answering my questions.

Guide: That's fine, but I'm sorry, we're out of time so we have to cancel the tour!

THE JAPANESE SALARYMAN

The typical, middle-class, white collar worker in Japan is known as the "salaryman." This is because he works for a salary which is normally paid once a month. He is considered to be the backbone of Japan's businessworld.

Let's take a look at the typical Japanese salaryman. He is married, has two children, works approximately 60 hours a week, and will stay with the same company all of his life. His life is his work and his work is his life.

The larger and more famous his company, the more likely it was that he graduated from a famous university, usually having studied economics or law. Nevertheless, his college training will probably be of little use in his company as most of the knowledge required will be learned "on the job."

Because of the incredible cost of land in the center of Japan's largest cities, he must often travel a minimum of one hour by train just to get to work. His wife sees him off early in the morning and is waiting with a warm dinner when he comes home, often as late as 11:00 PM. Needless to say, there is little time to spend with his wife and children each day. Many salarymen are looked upon as "weekend fathers."

Weekends are not always days of rest. Many salarymen are required to work one or two Saturdays each month. Even holidays which land on weekdays must be made up by working an extra Saturday that month. Summer vacations, although provided by the company, are rarely taken in full. Even though a salaryman may have up to nine days off, most wouldn't even consider taking their full allotment.

During rush hours the salaryman jams into a train where he passes the time reading (if he can find room to turn the pages), listening to a small radio with an ear phone, or catching up on his sleep. He wears conservative clothes and does nothing to stand out from the crowd.

Although English may be important in his business, the typical salaryman is unable to speak with any degree of confidence in spite of having studied English for a minimum of six years. He says he would like to have more practice in spoken English but finds little opportunity for it.

His company sometimes provides training in English and other critical skills after work. Unfortunately, his company also requires much overtime work, thus robbing the salaryman of any meaningful chance to study.

Although his starting salary is meager by Japanese standards, he gets a raise in salary each year to make up for the cost of living and to reflect his status in the seniority system. In addition to his salary, he receives many benefits including a commuter pass to and from work, free or subsidized housing, health insurance and a bonus equal to at least three or four month's salary twice a year. His taxes take about 10-15% of his pay each month.

Life at the company is not all work, however. Parties, outings, and other diversions are all offered to employees. And there is even an expense account. This nontaxable account is very important to the Japanese businessman because it is his principal source of entertainment.

Drinking at pubs and night clubs is the most popular form of entertainment in Japan. Wives are never invited to join in the entertainment, but the salaryman's wife doesn't seem to mind the frequent parties and nights out. In fact, many wives seem happy not to have their husbands in the way at home. The wife appears to regard the entire system as part of the natural order of things.

The Japanese salaryman is the pillar of success in *Japan, Inc.*

!) VOCABULARY -- Choose the answer (a,b,c,d) which best describes the underlined word.

a)   He is the underlined backbone of Japan's businessworld.

 a) chief support b) richest person c) poorest person d) worst worker

b)   Because of the incredible cost of land he must travel one hour to work.

 a) reasonable b) narrow c) unbelievable d) inexpensive

c)   He wears conservative clothes.

 a) colorful b) plain c) expensive d) political

d)   His starting salary is meager by Japanese standards.

 a) enthusiastic b) selfish c) insufficient d) normal

e)   Parties and other diversions are all offered to employees.

 a) benefits b) foods c) bonuses d) amusements

2) CONTENT -- According to the article,

a)   The salaryman

 a) works too hard and receives too little money.
 b) has a lonely and miserable wife and children.
 c) is the most important worker in Japan.
 d) spends too much time at work and entertaining.

b)   The salaryman's main form of entertainment comes from

 a) his company's English class budget.
 b) the company's nontaxable entertainment fund.
 c) his wife and children.
 d) frequent parties and nights out.

c)   The salaryman's wife

 a) objects to her husband's busy schedule and night life.
 b) dislikes living so far from the center of the city.
 c) is happy he receives a big bonus.
 d) doesn't mind if he is not at home very often.

d)   The typical salaryman

 a) is a college graduate.
 b) has too many holidays.
 c) plays and drinks too much.
 d) has an unhappy wife and children.

QUESTIONS FOR DISCUSSION

How are you different from the Japanese salaryman in this story? What kind of benefits does your company offer you? What are your working hours and overtime hours? How does your wife (or spouse) feel about your schedule? Do you think that *your life is your work and your work is your life*? Why? What kind of entertaining does your company do? What do you do afterward? How would you like to change your work life?

Name the following items by writing their English names in the blank spaces.

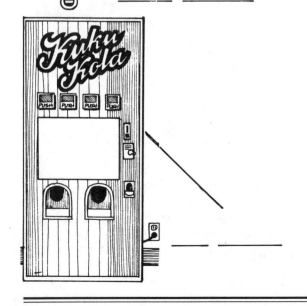

COMPARING BUSINESS PRACTICES AND CUSTOMS

American companies differ in many ways from those in other countries. Differences show up in the way desks are arranged to the way business clients are entertained. Use the following chart to discuss ways business is done in the U.S. versus in your country.

SUBJECT	YOUR COUNTRY	THE UNITED STATES
EXERCISE	Many companies and factories start the day by having the employees exercise together. What is the custom in your country?	Americans don't like the idea of exercising together at work. Can you imagine why?
STARTING & QUITTING TIMES	It is not uncommon in many countries for the average worker to come in one or two hours early and leave two to three hours after office hours. What are your working hours?	The typical American worker will "punch in" as close to starting time and "punch out" as close to quitting time as possible. Americans tend to be clock watchers.
STAGGERED HOURS & LUNCHES	Explain the average starting time for office jobs, factory work, and other jobs in your country. When and how long are lunch breaks? In your country what do people do during lunch breaks?	In large cities where traffic and parking are problems, the work hours are sometimes staggered. Lunch usually lasts 30 minutes to one hour.
VACATIONS & HOLIDAYS	Many countries almost close down at certain times of the year for vacations. Almost everyone takes his vacation at the exact same time. Also, in some countries, workers must work an extra day if they didn't work on a holiday. Describe the system in your country.	Most Americans take a two-week vacation sometime during the summer. Many companies have different employees take vacations at different times so that the office will remain open at all times. Workers also have many three-day weekends.
LUNCH MENUS	Does your company have an employee's cafeteria with a set menu at inexpensive prices? In some countries this is very common. What does the average worker eat for lunch in your country?	Most Americans bring their own lunches to work. Most "brown bag" it. Others eat out at "fast food" restaurants or buy food from vending machines.
PAY SCALES	How are pay scales set in your country? Is it by age, job skills, seniority, or government edict? Tell how pay is determined in your job. What are typical salaries ? Is there a minimum wage?	Pay is most often determined by the skill involved or the person's ability and experience. Talent is more important than age. Seniority is common in many labor union contract and government jobs. Minimum wages are set by Uncle Sam.

COMPARING BUSINESS PRACTICES AND CUSTOMS

SUBJECT	*YOUR COUNTRY*	*THE UNITED STATES*
TAXES	Are taxes in your country at the high or low end of the scale? In some places taxes take more than 50% of a worker's salary while in other countries taxes are low. What percentage do you pay? What do people in your country think about taxes and government?	No matter how high or low taxes are, people will complain about them. Federal, state, and local taxes add up to about 25%-35% of the average worker's salary. Many states also have sales taxes which take an additional 4-8%.
HIRING NEW EMPLOYEES	In some countries, new employees are hired only once a year. Large companies recruit primarily at big universities. Describe in detail how and where you were recruited or hired by your company. Why did you choose this company?	Most small companies recruit locally through the newspaper or private and public employment agencies. Word-of-mouth is also common. Large companies recruit at many colleges and universities throughout the year.
QUITTING & FIRING	Does your company offer a guaranteed lifelong employment system? Do most people work for the same company all their lives? Tell about quitting and firing in your country.	Many companies will lay off or fire employees if there is a slowdown or if the worker is incompetent. Workers often quit to find better jobs elsewhere.
RAIDERS	Is corporate raiding common in your country? Do big companies try to "steal" workers from rival companies? How common is this practice in your country or company?	Many large companies often try to persuade skilled or influential employees at other companies (usually rivals) to work for them.
BONUSES	Did you know that bonuses in some countries can equal almost one year's salary? Is there a bonus system in your company? How much does the average worker in your company receive and how often are bonuses paid?	Bonuses in the United States go mainly to CEO's and other "big wigs" who can show a profitable "bottom line." Most workers do receive a small bonus (usually $25 or a turkey) at Christmas.
OTHER BENEFITS	What other benefits does your company offer it's employees? Health insurance? Commuter passes? Housing allowance? Vacation villas?	Most American companies also provide the worker with good health insurance benefits, pension plans, sick leave, and vacations.

SUBJECT	YOUR COUNTRY	THE UNITED STATES
ENTERTAINING	Entertaining clients is, in some countries, the most important part of business negotiating. In fact, the entertainment budget is sometimes the largest item in some companies' budgets. Tell about entertaining clients in your country.	Important clients are often invited to formal dinners at expensive restaurants or at the home of a company executive. Wives are usually included. What do you think of the American way?
ROLE OF THE EXECUTIVE WIFE	In some countries women are never included in business discussions or even business entertaining. Wives are never included in company functions except occasional trips. What are the general feelings about involving wives in business dealings in your country?	The executive wife is very important because she is looked upon as the chief support for her husband. Often she is the hostess at parties held by the company to entertain clients. The impression an executive's wife makes on a customer is very important.
WOMEN EXECUTIVES	Is the women's movement having a major impact in your country? Are women encouraged to work out of the home? Are they discriminated against? Where are they having their biggest success? What do you think of women in business?	The number of women CEOs, lawyers, doctors, journalists, and other professionals is increasing tremendously year by year. Although women, on average, earn less than men earn, their economic and political power is increasing.
AFTER WORK	What do you usually do after work? How often do you go out with your fellow workers? Where do you go? How much do you spend? What does your spouse think of your after-work activities?	Most Americans go home right after work. A few might go out, but because both partners in most families now work, child-rearing and household chores must be shared.

ASSIGNMENT:	Make a list of things that are very unique to the business world in your country.
	Explain which customs would be very beneficial to other countries and which ones would probably only work in your country.
	Talk about mistakes foreign businessmen make in trying to do business in your country and how they should avoid them.
	Discuss why some foreign businesses in your country have been successful and why others have failed.

THE FACTORY WORKER

VOCABULARY

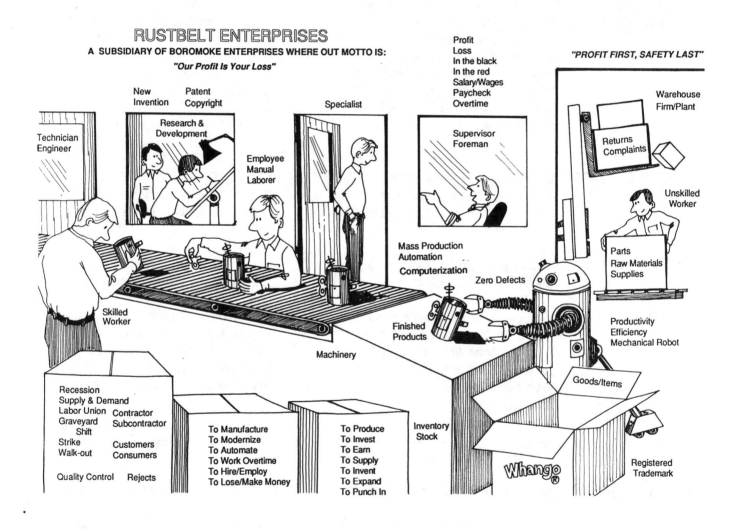

1) *Dictionary Study* -- Be able to tell the differences between the following kinds of workers.

- a) unskilled worker
- b) manual laborer
- c) blue collar worker
- d) skilled worker
- e) specialist
- f) technician

2) *Relationships* -- Describe the relation between the following word groups.

- a) raw materials-parts / machines / finished products / customers

- b) research & development (R&D) / assembly line / mechanical robot / quality control / rejects

- c) to hire / to produce / supply & demand
  - 1) to be laid off
  - 2) to work overtime

- d) inventor / invention / patent (copyright) / registered trademark / market

3) *Homonym Practice* -- The vocabulary page contains a number of words that have two or more meanings. List those meanings in the spaces below.

firm: _____   firm: _____

plant: _____   plant: _____

manual: _____   manual: _____

goods: _____   good: _____

profit: _____   prophet: _____

4) *General Questions for Discussion*

- a) What kind of raw materials does your factory purchase? From where?

- b) What kind of machinery is used in your job?

- c) What is your company's motto?

- d) What is your definition of "Safety First"?

- e) Can you give an example of someone who put "Profit First, Safety Last"?

to be laid off	=	to be dismissed; to lose one's job
to get a raise	=	to receive an increase in salary
to break down	=	to stop functioning; to stop moving
to be short of	=	to lack something

REWRITES: *Rewrite the following sentences by replacing the underlined words with the correct idiom.*

1) Because of the recession, he lost his job at the automobile factory.

2) Even though the cost of living has increased, the workers didn't receive an increase in salary.

3) When their computer stopped functioning, they were unable to check their inventory.

4) Our company lacks capital, so we will be unable to expand our operations.

FREE RESPONSE: *Answer the following questions with an appropriate response.*

1) Why are so many people being laid off in the (_____) industry?

2) If you don't get a raise this year, what will you do?

3) When (_____) breaks down, what do you do?

4) If a company is constantly short of money, what can it do to solve the problem?

5) If your company was short of cash and was unable to give you a raise (or bonus), what would you do?

FREE COMPLETION: *Complete the following sentences with an original ending.*

1) When the owners realized that the company was seriously short of capital. . .

2) Over 10,000 workers were laid off at that factory this year due to. . .

3) When the union was unable to get a raise for its members. . .

4) Because so many of that company's machines break down. . .

YOU TRY IT! *On a separate sheet of paper, make an original story using the new idioms.*

WORD FIND

Try to find each of the words from the list at the right in the box below. Some of the words are written horizontally, some backwards, some upside down, and some vertically.

engineer
computerize
specialist
robot
zero defects
machinery
firm
forklift
demand
copyright
technician
complaints
graveyard
supervisor
salary
hire
rejects
expand
invest
earn
return
supply
fire
loss
patent
shift
market
blue collar
goods
parts

```
A B C D E F G H I J K L M N O P Q R S T
B C O F E A R N E D C B U A Z S Y X P W
C R P I U M T S R Q P O N M L U K J E V
D E Y R X W A V U S T N I A L P M O C U
E T R E A U T N S R Q P O O O E T I I T
F U I G B V P O D M N K N J S R N I A S
G R G R A V E Y A R D V U T S V S H L R
H N H H C W Q W D C M E P B E I R G I R
I D T E C H N I C I A N A S J S Q F S Q
J E I A D X B X E N N G T H I O P E T E
K X J B E Y L Y F V A I E I H R O D A Z
L P K C F R U Z A E G N N F G N G C B I
M A C H I N E R Y N E E T T F T O B O R
N N L I G Z C J R T R E F S E M O B P E
O D M R I F O A E B C R I P D L D A O T
P E N E H I L J K C S A L A R Y S Z N U
Q A L D E F L G H I T J K R L M N Y M P
R F O P Q R A L O S S R T U V W X L M
S G H I M A R K E T J K O S U P P L Y O
T U V W X Y Z E R O D E F E C T S A B C
```

ACROSS

1) Materials needed to run a business
8) Primary source of energy for most factories
10) Not an amateur, a_____
11) Workers' organizations that negotiate with the factory management
13) Room or building in which a business person works
14) Calculate
19) "Send it as _____ as possible."
20) _____- skilled workers have little ability
21) Protection for inventors
23) "We are selling $100,000 per year, but as for profit, we are _____ only $9,000."
24) "During the strike, there was a walk -_____."
26) "I needed money, _____ I got a loan."
27) Not permanent
28) Los Angeles abbreviation
29) _____ paper basket
31) Mechanical "person"
33) "Let's write a business _____."
35) "Work hard _____ you'll be fired."
36) Where some employees go to drink after work
37) Night work period

DOWN

2) "They predict prices will go _____."
3) "If we don't make a _____ we'll be in the red."
4) Post Office abbreviation.
5) A person who risks money by putting it into a business or project
6) A contract used for carrying out a previous contract
7) Company
8) "Be _____ time."
9) "Is this feasible? No, it _____."
12) Data processor/ pc
15) "_____ more time"
16) "Whenever he goes to the bank, he_____ in money."
17) Same as 11 across
18) A person who is an expert at designing machines
22) Hire
25) United Airlines abbreviation
30) "Smoke filters help keep the _____ clean."
32) "Workers earn extra $ by working _____ - time."
33/35) "If a business fails, we must_____ _____ workers."
34) Equal Rights Amendment abbreviation
36) The root form of the words "is" and "are."

A TOUR OF THE FACTORY

Guide: Good afternoon. Welcome to our factory.
                Before we begin, do you have any questions?

Visitor: Yes, how large is this plant?

Guide: _____

Visitor: What do you manufacture here?

Guide: _____

Visitor: How many people work at this plant?

Guide: _____

Visitor: What percentage are blue collar workers?
                White collar workers? Women workers?

Guide: _____

Visitor: Where are your other plants?

Guide: _____

Visitor: What do they produce?

Guide: _____

Visitor: What is your job at this factory?

Guide: _____

Visitor: What benefits does this company offer its employees?

Guide: _____

Visitor: (The visitor may make up any other pertinent questions.)

Guide: Now, if you'll come this way we will begin our tour.

(The guide should give an actual tour of the plant or company.)

EDWARD DEMING: THE FATHER OF QUALITY CONTROL

W. EDWARD DEMING is a name almost unknown to most Americans. Yet in Japan, Deming's name is a household word. Not until the late 1970's and early 1980's when American businesses realized that customers were buying foreign cars and goods not only because of lower prices, but because of higher quality, did American industrialists finally start listening to this expert on quality control. He was, as the Bible says, *a prophet without honor in his own country*.

Mr. Deming strongly criticized the management class of American industry. He once stated, "The one thing we must never export is American management--at least to friendly countries ." He blamed American CEOs, business schools, and banks for stressing the "*bottom line*" and bonuses rather than customer satisfaction and quality products. He noted that industries rewarded those who maximized production and minimized costs, but they rarely rewarded efforts to improve quality.

He told factory managers that they had become strangers on their own factory floors, that their problems were of their own making. He believed that poor quality is 85% a management problem and 15% a worker problem.

Nominated for a Nobel Prize, Mr. Deming is considered by many to be the father of the third wave of the industrial revolution. The first wave was brought about by the mechanized factory thanks to Eli Whitney; the second was the mass production line started by Henry Ford; the third is the revolution of Edward Deming, using statistical controls to improve quality.

Deming's science, that of statistical quality control, is designed to tell a manufacturer whether he is buying from the right suppliers and whether the products coming down the assembly line are reaching the highest quality possible.

He was particularly critical of all-purpose business executives who come right out of business school with expertise in finance but none in the final product. He questioned whether they are in business just to make the biggest profit in the shortest amount of time or whether they are there to make a product with true excellence. A very important question he asked was, "Who can put a price on a satisfied customer and who can figure out the cost of a dissatisfied customer?"

It was in Japan in 1950 that Deming was asked to give his first series of lectures on quality control to top Japanese engineers and it is the Japanese who are Deming's prize students. Since 1951, the highest honor an industrialist in Japan can receive has been the Deming Prize, awarded to the company which produces the highest level of quality.

He summed up his views on the future of American industry with these words. "We in America will have to be more protectionist or more competitive. If we are to become more competitive, then we have to begin with our quality."

VOCABULARY
Circle the letter of the word or phrase that is the closest in meaning to the underlined word or phrase.

1) In Japan, Deming's name is a <u>household</u> word.

   a) *commonly used*   b) *used by every housewife*
   c) *used only in the home*   d) *kept in every house*

2) He was a <u>prophet</u> without honor in his own country.

   a) *a Christian*   b) *a person who sees and predicts the future*
   c) *a person who benefits*   d) *a believer*

3) He blamed...banks for stressing the "<u>bottom line</u>"...

   a) *end of the line*   b) *profit or loss statement*
   c) *lowest part*   d) *point farthest from the front*

4) It is the Japanese who are Deming's <u>prize</u> students.

   a) *most rewarded*   b) *richest*
   c) *surprised*   d) *best*

CONTENT
Circle the letter of the correct answers to the following questions derived from the reading.

1) When did most American manufacturers begin listening to Mr. Deming?

   a) In the 1950's
   b) In 1951
   c) In the late 1970's and early 1980's

2) What is the criteria for receiving the Deming Prize?

   a) Being an expert on quality control
   b) Producing a product of the highest quality
   c) Using statistics in quality control

3) What is the meaning of "statistical quality control"?

   a) Stressing the bottom line to maximize production and minimize costs
   b) Making the biggest profit in the shortest amount of time with fewer employees
   c) Informing the maker through statistics whether the products are of the highest quality possible

DISCUSSION POINTS

1) Why do you think it took so long for the Americans to listen to Mr. Deming?
2) Explain the phrase "A prophet without honor in his own country."
3) What does it mean, "managers had become strangers on their own factory floors"?
4) Expound on the question, "Who can put a price on a satisfied customer and who can figure out the cost of a dissatisfied customer?"
5) In what areas has your company excelled in quality control or customer satisfaction?

You received the following notice today from your supervisor.
Write a letter to the factory manager telling why you should not be laid off.

LAY OFF NOTICE

Dear Employee:

Because of the recent recession caused by the ————————— , orders to our company have fallen off drastically. Unfortunately, as a result, we have to lay off 50% of the assembly line workers. Your last day of work will be this Friday. Please pick up your paycheck at the payroll office on that day.

We're sorry to have to lay you off at this time. If you have any comments about this situation, please send them to us in writing by using the form below.

Thank you for your efforts here at *Rust Belt Enterprises.*

Sincerely,

The Manager

Dear Manager:

_____

_____

_____

_____

_____

_____

_____

FLEX TIME

With more and more married couples working, one serious problem has been how to take care of the children until school starts and after school lets out. One answer to this problem is flexible working hours. Some companies and many government offices are giving employees the choice of coming in early or working late in order to take care of other responsibilities or to take advantage of more leisure time.

With such a schedule, the father could take care of the children until they left for school and the mother would be home at about the same time the children were arriving home from school.

At most companies, all the workers must be in their places of work during the core hours of 10 AM to 3 PM, minus a one-hour lunch break. Employees may come in as early as 7 AM or as late as 10 AM and work until 4 PM or as late as 6 PM. All workers must decide on a schedule and stick to it. In addition, if a worker was on a 40-hour workweek before the change, that worker would have to continue to work 40 hours a week.

Because change is often hard to accept or adjust to, many companies have tried out flex time and then allowed the workers to vote whether to continue the system after an initial trial period.

One argument against flex time is that it makes it difficult for managerial supervision to be available at all times. Another is that this system could disrupt continuity of work, unless vital people such as secretaries' schedules were staggered.

QUESTIONS FOR DISCUSSION:

1) What is flex time?

2) In what kind of industries would this system work best? Worst?

3) What is *core time* at your company?

4) Who would this system serve best---men or women?

5) Would you personally like to work flexible hours? Why or why not?

6) What are the advantages or disadvantages of this system for management?

A WORKER'S LIFE
Company Bulletin Board

VOCABULARY

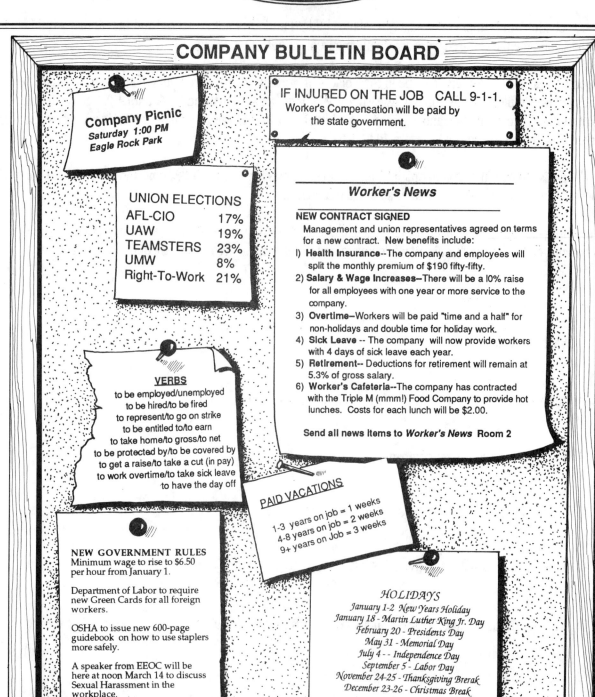

COMPANY BULLETIN BOARD

Company Picnic
Saturday 1:00 PM
Eagle Rock Park

IF INJURED ON THE JOB   CALL 9-1-1.
Worker's Compensation will be paid by
the state government.

UNION ELECTIONS

AFL-CIO	17%
UAW	19%
TEAMSTERS	23%
UMW	8%
Right-To-Work	21%

Worker's News

NEW CONTRACT SIGNED
Management and union representatives agreed on terms
for a new contract. New benefits include:
1) **Health Insurance**--The company and employees will
   split the monthly premium of $190 fifty-fifty.
2) **Salary & Wage Increases**--There will be a 10% raise
   for all employees with one year or more service to the
   company.
3) **Overtime**--Workers will be paid "time and a half" for
   non-holidays and double time for holiday work.
4) **Sick Leave** -- The company will now provide workers
   with 4 days of sick leave each year.
5) **Retirement**-- Deductions for retirement will remain at
   5.3% of gross salary.
6) **Worker's Cafeteria**--The company has contracted
   with the Triple M (mmm!) Food Company to provide hot
   lunches. Costs for each lunch will be $2.00.

Send all news items to *Worker's News* Room 2

VERBS
to be employed/unemployed
to be hired/to be fired
to represent/to go on strike
to be entitled to/to earn
to take home/to gross/to net
to be protected by/to be covered by
to get a raise/to take a cut (in pay)
to work overtime/to take sick leave
to have the day off

PAID VACATIONS

1-3 years on job = 1 weeks
4-8 years on job = 2 weeks
9+ years on Job = 3 weeks

NEW GOVERNMENT RULES
Minimum wage to rise to $6.50
per hour from January 1.

Department of Labor to require
new Green Cards for all foreign
workers.

OSHA to issue new 600-page
guidebook on how to use staplers
more safely.

A speaker from EEOC will be
here at noon March 14 to discuss
Sexual Harassment in the
workplace.

HOLIDAYS
January 1-2 New Years Holiday
January 18 - Martin Luther King Jr. Day
February 20 - Presidents Day
May 31 - Memorial Day
July 4 - - Independence Day
September 5 - Labor Day
November 24-25 - Thanksgiving Brerak
December 23-26 - Christmas Break

1) What do the following acronyms stand for?

    a) UAW

    b) OSHA

    c) AFL-CIO

    d) UMW

2) Find out the origin of the word "teamster." What does it mean today?

_____

3) Find out the meaning of the term "right-to-work."
Find out which states have this law and what the advantages and disadvantages of the law are to workers.

_____

4) Questions for discussion about your job:

    a) What health insurance benefits do you have? How much do you pay for this insurance?

    b) How often do you receive a raise? How is the raise decided? (seniority? inflation?)

    c) What are you paid for overtime work? Do you work on holidays? Do you have to make up holidays?

    d) What is your company's sick leave policy?

    e) At what age can you retire? What are the standard benefits?

    f) What (if any) union represents you? What is your opinion of this union?

    g) What holidays do you get off each year?

    h) How long is your paid vacation? When do you take it? What do you do? Where do you go?

5) Questions about laws in your country:

    a) What is the minimum wage in your country? What kind of workers most often receive the minimum wage?

    b) What do foreigners need to work legally in your country? Where are most of the foreign workers from? How are they treated?

    c) If you are injured on the job and have to quit work, what help do you get from your government? How long does the help last?

to put (something) together	=	to assemble
to be something wrong* with (something)	=	to have a problem with (something)
to have the day off	=	to have a one-day rest from work; to have a holiday
to fall off (in + noun)	=	to decrease (in number or quality)

*(or to be something the matter with)

DIALOGUE: *Rewrite the following dialogue by replacing the underlined parts with the new idioms.*

> *Supervisor:* Excuse me, but I think there is a <u>problem</u> with this product.
>
> *Foreman:* You're right! Who <u>assembled</u> it?
>
> *Supervisor:* I don't know, but perhaps this is why our sales are <u>decreasing</u>.
>
> *Foreman:* You're probably right. We seem to be short of workers who care about quality.
>
> *Supervisor:* Right! All they want is higher pay and to have more <u>holidays</u>

TRUE-FALSE: *Answer the following statements as to whether they are true or false in your opinion.*

1) If workers do not have two days off a week, their efficiency will fall off.

2) Even if something is not put together well, customers will buy it.

3) If something is wrong with the products you buy, you can always get a refund or an exchange.

4) Political problems in (name a country) are causing a fall-off in production of (name a commodity).

FREE RESPONSE: *Answer the following questions using the new idioms in this lesson.*

1) How many days off do you have each (week, month, year)? What do you do when you have the day off?

2) What do you enjoy putting together? What would you like to try putting together?

3) If something is wrong with your (name an item) who do you call?

4) If (production, efficiency, quality control, sales, etc.) falls off in your company, what happens?

YOU TRY IT! *On a separate sheet of paper, make an original story using the four new idioms in this lesson.*

THE AMERICAN WORKER
Recommended reading time: 4-6 minutes depending on level of class

1   Although the United States still leads the world in economic productivity and GNP, there are some major differences
2   in American working habits compared with those of many other industrial giants. For example, it is very common
3   for Americans to change jobs during their lifetimes. In fact, many companies try to hire people from other companies
4   by offering better salaries and benefits. If a worker stays with the same company all of his life, some people may
5   think that worker has no ambition to strive for something better.

6   Salaries are quite high in the U.S. compared with many countries, but there are some definite disadvantages too.
7   Taxes are relatively high in spite of huge tax cuts and efforts at tax reform which took place in the 1980s. A worker
8   pays federal taxes, Social Security (about 7.3%), state taxes, and even city taxes in some areas. In addition to these
9   taxes which are deducted directly from his paycheck, the American worker in most states has to pay state sales
10 taxes (usually 4 to 8%) on whatever he buys, property tax if he owns a home, gasoline tax and other taxes. Altogether,
11 a typical worker pays about 35-40% of his salary to the government.

12 Overtime is not common in the United States because it is too expensive for the employer who must pay the
13 employee "time and a half" or doubletime for any overtime work. In spite of the higher pay offered, many employees
14 shun overtime, preferring to spend the time in leisure activities or with their families.

15 There are usually two coffee breaks during the day--one in mid-morning and one in mid-afternoon. During these
16 breaks, workers may relax, eat or chat with each other. Lunch time is a minimum of 30 minutes and a maximum
17 of 60 minutes long. Most blue collar and many white collar workers take their own lunches to work in a paper
18 sack, a custom known as "brown bagging." A bagged lunch typically consists of a sandwich, fruit, chips, dessert,
19 and sometimes hot soup and a hot or cold drink. A male worker's lunch is most likely made by his wife. Fast food
20 establishments are the norm for workers who go out for lunch.

21 Working hours are from 8 AM to 5 PM with some variations. Most workers work only five days a week. Other than
22 retail stores in malls and supermarkets, most businesses are closed on Sundays.

23 Because most workers have to compete with each other for higher positions and better salaries, there is a lot of
24 competition to stand out at work. Seniority does not ensure better pay or a higher position in the company. People
25 are more likely to work as individuals than on teams.

26 Unfortunately, even if a worker has been very diligent and faithful to the company, he may be laid off in times of
27 recession or when a more efficient worker is hired. Most companies provide a pension or parting pay to the worker.

28 Government payments to the unemployed and to the retired are paid through unemployment compensation (state
29 administered) and Social Security (federally administered). These payments help the old and retired maintain a
30 fair standard of living in their old age. How would you like to be an American worker?

VOCABULARY TEST: *Choose the closest meaning (a, b, or c) of the underlined word from the story.*

1) *giants* (line 2)

      a) power   b) baseball team   c) countries

2) *deducted* (line 9)

      a) understood   b) reduced   c) subtracted

3) *shun* (line 14)

      a) avoid   b) hate   c) love

4) *typically* (line 18)

      a) sometimes   b) usually   c) never

5) *ensure* (line 24)

      a) provide   b) protect   c) guarantee

COMPREHENSION TEST: *Answer the following questions based on your understanding of the story.*

1) How do some companies try to attract workers from other companies?

      a) They pay higher taxes.
      b) They pay more unemployment compensation.
      c) They offer better salaries and benefits.

2) According to the story, which statement about taxes is correct?

      a) Americans pay fewer taxes than most other people.
      b) Americans pay more taxes than most other people.
      c) American salaries are high but taxes are high too.

3) According to this story, what sometimes happens to even diligent workers?

      a) They are laid off in times of recession.
      b) They bring their lunches in paper sacks.
      c) They like to spend their leisure time with their families.

4) What is true about the seniority system in the U.S.?

      a) Most companies provide seniors with a good pension.
      b) It does not ensure better pay or a higher position in the company.
      c) It is an individual system rather than a group one.

DISCUSSION QUESTIONS

1) Why do Americans change jobs often?

2) Do people in your country change jobs often? Why or why not?

3) What are the advantages and disadvantages of changing jobs often?

4) What kind of taxes do Americans pay? What kind do you pay?

5) Describe the social security system in the U.S. and in your country?

6) Why is overtime work unpopular with many American workers?

7) How do people in your country feel about overtime work?

8) What do workers do during coffee breaks? What is a coffee break called in your country?

9) How long is the lunch break in your country? Where do you eat?

10) What does *brown bagging* mean? How do you think it got its name?

11) What is a typical lunch in the U.S.? In your country?

12) How much do you normally pay if you eat out for lunch?

13) Why do Americans work as individuals? What are the advantages and disadvantages of this system?

14) When do you think a company is justified in *firing* a person?

15) At what age do most workers in your country retire?

16) What do most retirees do to occupy their time?

17) Which statement fits you best: *I work to live* or *I live to work* ?

DON'T SAY YES WHEN YOU MEAN NO

Most Americans, and most Westerners for that matter, are direct, candid, and frank. When most people say "no" they mean no. When they say "yes" they mean yes. They are not used to dealing with people who say yes but mean no. Here are some important hints to remember.

SAY NO IMMEDIATELY

If you know you or your company are not willing or able to do something for the client or potential customer, tell the person as soon as he asks. Don't waste his valuable time --and yours--saying yes when you have little or no intention of granting the request. Even worse, do not say "I'll think about it" when you have already rejected the proposal.

BE UP-FRONT

Instead of leading a person on, give a good reason why you will or will not be able to meet his or her requests. There is no need to give minute details as to why the request cannot be made, but the other party should be told up-front that his request is either out of the question or a distinct possibility.

BE FRIENDLY

You may want to do business with this person at a later time, so be sure to maintain a cordial atmosphere in the business dealings. Business people can be friendly and direct at the same time. Americans will feel betrayed if the friendliness is just a facade, however.

GIVE SOME KIND OF TIME FRAMEWORK

Americans feel frustrated not knowing when or how long it will be before a decision can be made or an agreement can be reached. Even though business dealings in your company and your country may take much longer than would be the norm in the United States, let your American client know about how long it will be before the next step in the negotiations or decision-making process takes place. Americans are very calendar conscious.

PUT THE BALL IN THE OTHER PERSON'S COURT

This phrase means to let the other person make the decision. Give the responsibility to the other person so that you will not be the one who has to say no. If your client wants you to make certain unacceptable concessions, tell him the only way you can do it is if he will make certain concessions that you desired which he felt were unacceptable. The key is to get people to see it may be in their best interest for you to say no.

SECTION 6

English For The Financier

BANKING & FINANCE
Money Matters

FIRST INTERNATIONAL BANK
*"We stretch dollars,
not the truth at FIB."*

International Exchange
Call Toll Free 1-800-555-0001 for the latest information on international currency exchange rates.

Safe Deposit Box
Guaranteed security for your valuables for only $15 per month.

Fireproof Vault and Safe
We've never lost a penny to fire or flood at FIB, and our guards are on 24-hour duty.

Overdraft Protection
Guard against bounced checks. For only $0.50 per month you can qualify for $300 overdraft protection.

ATMs & Cash Cards
24-Hour service at all branches allows you to withdraw or deposit money any day, and at any hour.

Drive-Thru Teller
Our drive-thru teller is open from 7 AM to 6 PM Monday through Friday and 9 AM -12 AM on Saturday.

High Interest Rates on Savings
No bank offers higher rates on passbook accounts than FIB. Ask about our IRAs too.

Free Checking
Keep a balance of $300 and there will be no monthly fee.

M.T. Pockets
321 Elm Street
Salem. OR 00777

_____ 19_____

Check #: _____
24-1234 / 3230

Pay to the order of _____ $ [   ]

_____ dollars

Memo: _____ Signed: _____

0421:345676::0098::12AB   First International Bank / Salem

DENOMINATIONS

BILLS

hundreds ($100)
fifties ($50)
twenties ($20)
tens ($10)
fives ($5)
twos ($2)
ones ($1)

COINS

silver dollars ($1)
half-dollars ($0.50)
quarters ($0.25)
dimes ($0.10)
nickels ($0.05)
pennies ($0.01)

FIRST INTERNATIONAL BANK

CHECK GUARANTEE CARD

M.T. POCKETS
0421:345676::0098::12AB

FIRST INTERNATIONAL BANK · STATEMENT

DATE	TRANSACTION	AMOUNT	BALANCE
3/1	deposit	17.64	348.19
3/3	withdrawal	300.00	48.19
3/7	withdrawal	58.19	-10.00
3/8	withdrawal	60.00	-70.00
3/8	penalty	15.00	-85.00

PLEASE NOTE: *YOUR ACCOUNT HAS BEEN CLOSED DUE TO INSUFFICIENT FUNDS!*

1) Be able to identify and give the formal names and nicknames for each coin listed below.

a) 1¢
b) 5¢
c) 10¢
d) 25¢
e) 50¢
f) $1 (coins)

2) Reading dollar and cent amounts often confuses people from other countries. Try reading the following amounts as a native speaker would say them.

a) $1.50
b) $2.98
c) $20.05
d) $5.75
e) $3.25
f) $115.01

3) Change each verb below to a "personal" noun and tell what that person does.

EXAMPLE: to cash = a cashier (a cashier receives and pays out money)

a) to sign
b) to apply
c) to borrow
d) to pay
e) to insure
f) to lend
g) to rob
h) to embezzle

4) Change each noun below to its verb form and give its definition.

a) identification =
b) accountant =
c) signature =
d) insurance =
e) witness =

5) General Questions for Discussion

a) How much interest does your bank pay on a regular passbook account?

b) Why do you think Americans use checking accounts?
What are the advantages and disadvantages?
Are checks commonly used in your country?

c) What are banking hours in your country?
What services are offered after banking hours?

d) What kind of identification and bank or credit cards do you carry?
What would you do if you lost them?

to count on (someone/thing)	=	to trust, to depend on, to rely on
to figure out	=	to understand, to solve
to keep track of (to lose track of)	=	to maintain a record of something; to forget
to spend (time, money, etc.) (on)	=	to use (time, money, etc.) (+ ing)

REWRITES: *Replace the underlined words with the most suitable new idiom.*

1) You can <u>depend on</u> that teller to give you fast, efficient service.

2) Even though I <u>used</u> a lot of time filling out the loan application, the bank refused to loan me even one red cent!

3) I can't <u>understand</u> that thief. He stole all the coins but none of the bills!

4) Do you <u>maintain a record</u> of your business expenses for the IRS?

FREE RESPONSE: *Answer the following questions using the correct idiom in your answer.*

1) What do you do when you can't figure out your (taxes, bank balance, cooking recipe, etc.)?

2) What do you spend your (salary, free time, etc.) on?

3) Who can you count on in times of trouble at home, work, etc.?

4) How do you keep track of (your friends, debts, people's phone numbers, etc.)?

FREE COMPLETION: *Complete the following sentences with an original ending.*

1) I can never figure out my bank balance because. . .

2) My (husband, wife, girlfriend) can't keep track of _____ because. . .

3) I want to spend more money on _____ but. . .

4) We were counting on (name) to lend us _____ , but. . .

5) Can you help me figure out how to. . .

6) I lost track of the number of times I. . .

7) If you don't spend more time on _____ you will. . .

8) Can I count on you to. . .

YOU TRY IT! *On a separate sheet of paper, make an original story using the new idioms.*

AT THE BANK

Customer: Excuse me. Where can I exchange this (foreign currency) for dollars?

Teller: Foreign exchange is at Window 8.

Customer: Thanks.

Customer: (At Window 8) Hi. Can I exchange (name of currency) here?

Teller: Sure. How much would you like to exchange?

Customer: Let's see. What's the exchange rate for _____ today?

Teller: It's _____ to a dollar.

Customer: You must be kidding. It was just _____ a week ago!

Teller: Sorry. What would you like to do?

Customer: I guess I'll exchange _____ .

Teller: Fine. That comes to _____ dollars and _____ cents. What denominations would you like?

Customer: Fifties, twenties, tens, fives, and ones please.

Teller: Here you are. (Counts out the money.) Thank you, sir.

Customer: Thank you.

SMALL CHANGE

Customer: Excuse me. Can you change this five-dollar bill for me?

Teller: You bet. Will five ones be all right?

Customer: No, I need some small change too.

Teller: No problem. How about 3 ones, 4 quarters, 6 dimes, 6 nickels, and 10 pennies?

Customer: Perfect. Thanks a million.

My pleasure. Come again.

Each student will pair up with a partner. One will act as the bank official and the other as the applicant. The bank official will ask the questions on the page and the applicant will answer without looking at the questions on the page.

BANK of the U.S.A.
Credit Card Application

NAME IN FULL *(last, first, middle)*:

HOME ADDRESS:

DATE OF BIRTH:

TELEPHONE *(home and work)*:

MARITAL STATUS *(single, married, divorced or separated)*:

NAME OF SPOUSE:

OF CHILDREN AT HOME:

PRESENT EMPLOYER:

ADDRESS: POSITION:

DATE OF HIRE: MONTHLY SALARY:

SPOUSE'S PRESENT EMPLOYER:

ADDRESS: POSITION:

DATE OF HIRE: MONTHLY SALARY:

NAME & ADDRESS OF BANK:

TYPE OF ACCOUNT *(checking, savings, loan)*:

ACCOUNT NUMBERS:

HOUSING *(own, rent or lease)*:

MONTHLY RENT / MORTGAGE: MORTGAGE HOLDER:

PURCHASE PRICE: PRESENT BALANCE:

CREDIT REFERENCES *(banks, credit cards, etc.)*:

DRESSING PROFESSIONALLY

As your company's representative, you will be establishing a first impression--favorable or unfavorable--by your words, actions, and your dress and grooming. Since first impressions are often lasting impressions, it is important to you and your company that you dress in a professional manner.

In the United States, most male corporate officials wear traditional dark blue or dark gray suits. Research has proven that these suits give the businessman the most credibility. White, long-sleeved cotton shirts with button-down collars also give a good impression and are usually best for comfort and durability.

The most widely accepted shoe style for males is the laced, plain-toe oxford, but plain and tasseled loafers are acceptable as well. Black, cordovan, and brown are all acceptable shoe colors for daytime business wear, but brown shoes are not normally worn with evening wear.

Black, brown, or navy blue cotton or nylon socks are recommended for the professional businessman. Socks should be long enough to cover the calf when you sit cross-legged. White socks are never worn with business suits.

Conservative colors and patterns are also most suitable for neckties. The necktie should reach to the middle of the belt buckle.

It is recommended that wallets be kept in the suit jacket breast pocket.

On single breasted suits, coats should be buttoned when standing and unbuttoned when you are seated.

For the corporate businesswoman, the most generally accepted look is the matched, skirted wool suit in colder temperatures and cotton or rayon in warmer temperatures. Dark, conservative colors are recommended. Hemlines should not reflect the most recent trend--the best skirt length is below the knees.

Shoes should be of good quality leather, comfortable, and easy to walk in. The best shoe is a closed toe pump with a medium heel. The shoe color should always be at least one shade darker than the hemline of the skirt.

Hair should always appear neat and controlled. Wild hairstyles may destroy the image that an aspiring professional is trying to convey.

Jewelry should be conservative and simple. Avoid wild earrings and bracelets.

Dress like a professional. Act like a professional. Be a professional.

DIRECTIONS

The class will be divided into two teams. Each team will receive $1000 in play money at the beginning of the game. Each team rolls one die and moves the number of spaces indicated. If a team lands on a square with two items, the team must use both of those items correctly in an English sentence within 60 seconds in order to receive the appropriate amount of money from the bank. (The teacher will be the banker). If the team fails, that amount is subtracted from the team's total and added to the vault. If a team lands on a square which indicates "receive" or "pay" cash, follow the instructions on that square. When both teams have gone around the board twice and reached the last square, the money totals will be added up; the team with the most money wins.

START	"RUBBER CHECK" "KEEP TRACK OF"	"WITHDRAW" "AMOUNT"	"THIEF" "ROB"	THE VAULT !!! collect all money from the vault!	INTEREST PAYMENT! bank pays 5% of all money you now have
Receive $100 interest	$35	$50	$25	collect "X"	collect "X"

THE VAULT

I.R.S. PENALTY! pay 5% of all of your money to the IRS pay "X"					SAVINGS MATURES! bank savings bond matures collect $50

| BANK MISTAKE! a bank error in your favor collect $50 | "TO CASH" "COUNTER CHECK" $30 | | | RETURN TO START! start over with extra money collect $100 | "APPLICATION" "OPEN AN ACCOUNT" $45 |

| | "GUARD" "VAULT" $25 | | | PREMIUMS DUE! insurance premiums are now due pay $50 | |

| "MONEY ORDER" "TELLER" $25 | "SAFETY DEPOSIT BOX" "IDENTIFICATION" $40 | | | "FIGURE OUT" "BALANCE" $30 | "JOINT ACCOUNTS" "TO SIGN" $60 |

| INCOME TAX! lose 10% of all of your money pay "X" | **PLACE ALL PAYMENTS HERE** | | | | "CHANGE" "A HUNDRED" $50 |

| DEPOSIT MATURES! certificate of deposit finally matures! collect $200 | | | | | "TO FILL OUT" "DEPOSIT SLIP" $100 |

| "DEPOSIT" "SAVINGS ACCOUNT" $30 | "CHECKBOOK" "SIGNATURE" $35 | BOUNCED CHECK! you write a rubber check pay $20 | GIFT! get money from the other team! receive $100 | BANK ROBBED! you lose money as well pay $200 | "PIGGY BANK" "TO ROB" $100 |

THE FINANCIAL INVESTOR
Stocks & Bonds

VOCABULARY

supply & demand	prosperity/bankruptcy	depression/recession
IRS	CEO	socialism/communism
IRA	GNP	wholesale/retail
analyst	investor	profit/loss
government regulation	legislation/tax laws	boom
tax shelter	(un)employment	Wall Street
inflation	free market/free enterprise	DJ (Dow Jones)
monopoly/cartel	crash	investment
blue-chip	penny stocks/OTC	stock(market)
bonds	multi-national	stockholder/broker
income tax	treasury notes	SEC
fiscal policy/monetary policy	panic	NYSE
bear market/bull market	speculation	capitalist

1) What do the following acronyms stand for?

a) I.R.S.

b) D.J.

c) S.E.C.

d) I.R.A.

e) G.N.P.

f) N.Y.S.E.

2) What is the opposite of. . .?

a) capitalism =

b) inflation =

c) boom =

d) blue-chip stocks =

e) employment =

f) profit =

g) wholesale =

h) supply =

3) General Questions for Discussion

a) What is the name of America's main financial district?

b) Give an example of the workings of supply and demand.

c) Name one or more foreign-based multi-national companies in your country. Name some from your country.

d) How does the monetary policy of the U.S. affect your country?

e) What is the unemployment rate in your country? In the U.S.?

f) What are some advantages and disadvantages of capitalism vs. communism?

4) Choose one blue-chip stock and one other non blue-chip stock of your choice from the newspaper and follow their progress for a week or more. Be prepared to report to the class on the progress of the stocks you choose.

5) If available, play a game of Monopoly® to introduce the students to the general workings of capitalism and real estate.

to be interested in (+ noun) (+ gerund)	=	to want (something); to want to (do)
to take over (+ noun)	=	to assume control of (something)
to sell out	=	to sell completely
to go from bad to worse	=	to get worse; to worsen
to call off	=	to cancel

REWRITES: Rewrite the following sentences using the new idioms in place of the underlined phrases.

1) My client wants to buy one thousand shares of blue-chip stock.

2) From what I understand, the shareholders are interested in assuming control of that near-bankrupt airline.

3) Market analysts are encouraging investors to sell all their stock in that industry before the economy worsens.

4) Panic buying and selling caused the Dow Jones to worsen.

5) They cancelled the merger of those two companies when the stockholders threatened to sue.

FREE RESPONSE: Answer the following sentences with an appropriate response.

1) Why is the situation in the (_____) industry going from bad to worse?

2) If the economy goes from bad to worse, what plans might your company (family, etc..) have to call off?

3) If I had stock in (_____), I would immediately sell out because. . .

4) Why are many governments interested in raising (or lowering) taxes?

5) What kind of industries are you (or your company) interested in taking over?

FREE COMPLETION: Complete the following sentence with an original ending.

1) They are selling out their interest in that multinational company in order to. . .

2) Unemployment seems to be going from bad to worse in the (_____) industry because. . .

3) The company president decided to call off plans to (_____) because. . .

4) Our company is interested in making an investment in (_____) because. . .

5) Government regulations do not allow some big companies to take over smaller companies because. . .

YOU TRY IT!! On a separate sheet of paper, make an original story using the new idioms in this lesson.

THE GREAT DEPRESSION (1929 - 1939)
Suggested Reading Time: 7-9 minutes

1   The Great Depression, which began in 1929 with the crash of the stock market and ended with the outbreak of
2   World War II, had an effect on the economy and politics of the United States that is still felt strongly today. In the
3   decade prior to the crash, the U.S. had been experiencing an economic boom. Henry Ford's Model T's were
4   rolling off the assembly lines, stock market speculation was widespread, and the nation was enjoying Republican
5   prosperity. The President, Calvin Coolidge, was a conservative who believed in laizzez-faire, or allowing business
6   activities to be conducted without government regulation. As a result, credit was loose and the economy was inflating.

7   Even before Republican Herbert Hoover was elected President in 1928, there were signs that the nation was heading
8   for economic difficulties. Industrial production and retail sales began to decline and construction was off. The
9   nation entered into a period of severe deflation, forcing many businesses to slow down their activities or call off
10 expansion plans.

11 As a result of the Crash of 1929, banks began to fail, stockholders lost millions of dollars overnight, companies
12 everywhere went bankrupt, and unemployment skyrocketed. By 1932, 25% of the labor force was out of work.
13 The effects of the depression were felt in almost every country of the world, but most severely in the industrialized
14 Western European nations of Germany and Great Britain.

15 World trade came to a near standstill as country after country put up trade barriers on imports and the Gold
16 Standard was abandoned. In Europe, totalitarian regimes began to come to power with promises of economic
17 programs that would lead their nations to supremacy in the world.

18 In the United States, President Hoover tried to use the powers of the government to solve the economic recession.
19 He raised duties on imports, authorized the government to purchase surplus farm products, cut taxes, liberalized
20 credit, increased public works spending, and asked business and labor leaders to maintain production, employment,
21 and pay scales.

22 Unfortunately, these policies were not sufficient to save the economy which went from bad to worse. By 1932,
23 hundreds of banks had failed, one quarter of the farmers had lost their farms, and factories throughout the nation
24 were shut down. In that same year the nation's voters turned to the Democratic candidate, Franklin D. Roosevelt,
25 to solve the severe depression. In his first speech as President, he told the people, "The only thing we have to fear
26 is fear itself."

27 In his first 100 days in office, Roosevelt had Congress pass legislation which reopened most of the banks, set up
28 an agriculture recovery program, provided more unemployment relief, gave the government power to supervise
29 securities, aided railroads, helped home owners pay their mortgages, and set up an industrial recovery program.

30 FDR's "New Deal" was America's first experiment with a government-controlled economy. It took nine years, until
31 the beginning of World War II, before the Depression actually ended, but the legislation, economic policies, and
32 political impact the Depression and the New Deal had on the United States still continue to this day.

DEFINITIONS 1: Choose the letter (a, b, c, or d) which best matches the meaning of the underlined word.

1) In the decade <u>prior</u> to the crash. . .(Line 3)

    a) before   b) after   c) about   d) into

2) The President. . .believed. . .that there should be few government <u>regulations</u>. (Line 6)

    a) politicians   b) businesses   c) rules   d) regards

3) Industrial production. . .began to <u>decline</u>. . .(Lines 9-10)

    a) improve   b) decide   c) go down   d) deflate

4) [Un]employment <u>skyrocketed</u>. (Line 13)

    a) was cloudy   b) was fast   c) inflated   d) went up rapidly

5) The effects. . .were felt. . .most <u>severely</u> in. . .Europe. . .(Lines 14-15)

    a) casually   b) violently   c) skillfully   d) easily

6) World trade came to a near <u>standstill</u>. . .(Line 17)

    a) stop   b) disaster   c) move   d) dislike

7) He raised <u>duties</u> on imports. . .(Line 21)

    a) responsibilities   b) barriers   c) taxes   d) the Gold Standard

8) [T]hese policies were not <u>sufficient</u> to save the economy. . .(Line 24)

    a) suffering   b) enough   c) magnificent   d) decent

9) [L]egislation. . .provided more unemployment <u>relief</u>. . .(Lines 29-30)

    a) depression   b) fever   c) aid   d) public works

10) FDR's New Deal was America's first <u>experiment</u>. . .(Line 33)

    a) bankruptcy   b) knowledge   c) candidate   d) trial

DEFINITIONS 2: *Choose the letter (a, b, c, or d) which best matches the definition below.*

1) *to buy and sell stocks with risk of loss and hope of profit through changes in market value*

   a) securities   b) speculate   c) authorized   d) failed

2) *allowing business activities to be conducted without government regulation*

   a) laizzez-faire   b) conservative   c) Republican   d) recovery

3) *made free or easier*

   a) authorized   b) failed   c) supervised   d) liberalized

4) *method or system of government which allows only one political party*

   a) Republican   b) Democratic   c) totalitarian   d) regime

5) *something that prevents or controls progress or movement*

   a) barrier   b) surplus   c) mortgage   d) voter

6) *to keep up; retain; continue*

   a) to decline   b) to maintain   c) to solve   d) to shut down

COMPREHENSION QUESTIONS

1) This article can be summed up by saying that:

   a) The only thing we have to fear is fear itself.
   b) The New Deal still continues today.
   c) The U.S. economy moved from one of laizzez-faire to one of much government control.

2) What one political side effect of the depression was felt in some foreign countries?

   a) They began World War II to end the Depression.
   b) Totalitarian regimes began to come to power.
   c) The Republicans were ousted by the Democrats.

3) What were some of the signs that the U.S. was heading toward a depression?

   a) bank failures, stock losses, and bankruptcies
   b) decline in industrial production, fewer sales, drop in construction
   c) election of Republican Herbert Hoover

4) According to the story, the New Deal can best be described as:

   a) The first experiment the U.S. had with a controlled economy.
   b) FDR's legislation to help the Republican party.
   c) The period from 1929 to World War II.

LEARNING ABOUT OTHER COUNTRIES

As the world grows smaller in size because of advances in transportation and communications, financial investments overseas continue to increase. The following list of questions should be asked of yourself or anyone from your company who will be living, studying, or doing business abroad.

*Note to teacher: Assign students different categories and have them present oral reports on their findings. Focus on countries where the class members reside, may reside, or where their companies do business.

Politics

1) Who are the current leaders of the country? How are they elected?

2) Name the major political parties.

3) What kind of legislature do they have?

4) What kind of penalties are there for disobeying the law?

5) Are corruption and bribery a part of the government and business?

6) Can women vote and hold political office?

The Country

1) How many (if any) states, provinces, prefectures, etc. are there in the country?

2) What are the main cities? Their populations? Main industries? Main problems?

3) What is their basic history? Their relationship to other counties? Date of independence?

4) What are the different areas of climate and geography?

Roles of Men & Women

1) Are male and female workers equally esteemed?

2) Are there different roles for men and women in business? Equal pay for equal work?

3) What is the social position of women?

Religion

1) Is there a state religion?

2) How does religion influence the people?

3) What are the main religions?

4) What are some differences or conflicts between your beliefs and the beliefs of the main religion(s) in this country?

Food

1) What kinds of foods are eaten? Which are taboo?

2) What beverages (if any) are served at business meetings?

3) What is standard eating etiquette? What manners must be observed?

4) Is there a tipping system? If so, describe it.

5) Can you drink the water from the tap? If not, what do you drink?

Health

1) What medical facilities are available?

2) What do you need to be careful of to maintain good health?

Education

1) Is education free? Compulsory? To what age?

2) How are children disciplined at school? At home? Who does the disciplining?

3) Is there much competition to enter college?

4) How important is the name of the college a student attends?

Daily Life

1) What are some courtesies you should observe?

2) How do people greet each other?

3) Is gift-giving a custom? What is given and when?

4) Do colors or numbers have a special meaning? (Lucky or unlucky?)

5) How many days a week do people work? What are the work hours? Lunch hours?

6) Is alcohol permitted? What is drunk at business and social functions?

7) What kinds of programs are not permitted on TV, in the movies, on video?

8) Do people commonly use servants?

Their Attitude Toward You

1) What is the relationship between your country and this country? How has it been in the past five years? What is the future outlook?

2) Are people from your country liked or disliked? For what reasons?

3) Is there a large expatriate community? Do they all live in the same area?

4) What is your attitude toward the people?

5) What is their attitude toward you? Do they feel superior? Inferior?

Non-Verbal Communication

1) Will they understand your non-verbal communication (body language) ?

2) Is there any body language you should avoid?

Social Structure

1) What are the class divisions and percentages?

2) What are the ethic divisions and percentages?

3) Is there any discrimination? Against whom?

4) What is their attitude toward foreigners?

5) What are the major occupations of the people?

6) What is the average family size? Is birth control practiced?

7) Is crime a problem? What kind?

8) Is the group more important than the individual members of the group?

Business & Social Customs

1) What are some important business values?

2) Should you invite business colleagues to your home? Will you be invited to their homes?

3) Is punctuality important? When can you be late?

4) How does a company reward workers? Higher pay? Bonuses?

5) Is smoking common? What is the public attitude toward smoking and drinking?

Newspapers & The Media

1) Which newspapers are most popular? Is there censorship in the country?

2) What are the most popular newspapers and TV stations?

3) Are any cable networks not permitted?

4) Is pornography in the media common?

Sports

1) Is there a national sport?

2) What sports are most popular?

3) How does the country do at the Olympics? What events are they strong in?

SECTION 7

English For Negotiating

ALL ABOUT NEGOTIATING

---

ne·go·ti·ate

1   vi, vt (with sb)

discuss, confer, in order to come to an agreement:
We've decided to <u>negotiate</u> with the employers about our wage claims.

2   sth (with sb)

arrange by discussion; a sale / a loan / a treaty / peace.

Everybody negotiates all the time, at work, at home, and as a consumer. For some it is easy, but others are very uncomfortable with negotiating.

Most people think of negotiations as formal proceedings that occur under high pressure. In reality, people are negotiating all the time. Negotiating is, in fact, an important life skill.

Negotiating is a means of making decisions with other people in a civilized way. In some countries, negotiating is an art form and initial offers are never accepted. In other countries, there may be little or no room for negotiating.

As you read through this section, consider the do's and don'ts of negotiating with Americans. Remember that you may not necessarily be able to use negotiating skills from your own country and culture.

This is a perfect time to remember the wise proverb, "When in Rome, do as the Romans do."

10 TIPS FOR BETTER NEGOTIATING

Read through and discuss each item below. Compare each negotiating tip to methods used in your country.

1) **Everything is negotiable.** You can ask, offer, counter offer and suggest alternatives.

2) **Be prepared.** Knowledge is power in negotiating. When you know a lot about the deal, and understand the other side's position well, you will probably get exactly what you want. Ask, "What do they need?" "What pressures are they under?" "What are their options?"

3) **Aim high.** Ask for more than you expect to receive, and offer less than you are actually willing to pay. Be an optimist, but know when to stop. Establish your limit, and go no further.

4) **Be patient.** This is very difficult for Americans who want to get everything over with quickly. Whoever has more time and is more flexible has the advantage.

5) **Focus on satisfaction.** It is important that both sides feel satisfied. Don't confuse needs with wants. Remember that their position is what they <u>say</u> they want; their basic interests are what they really <u>need</u> to get.

6) **Don't make the first move.** Whenever possible, get the other party to make the first move. They may ask for less than you think. If you make the first move, you may give away more than is necessary.

7) **Don't accept the first offer.** If you do, the other negotiator will think they could have done better. Believe it or not, they will feel more satisfied if you turn down the first offer. Then when you do say "yes," they will feel that they have gotten the best deal possible. Be willing to ask, "Is this the best deal you can offer me?"

8) **Smile even when you are saying "No."** Speaking angrily will weaken your position. Learn to say no firmly while still being polite.

9) **Show the value of your offer.** If you make a win-win offer, make sure the other side recognizes the benefits and advantages of your offer. Don't assume that the other side understands the benefits to them.

10) **Be willing to walk away.** When you know your limit and are willing to walk away with no deal, you're in a strong position. Occasionally you might lose a deal, but in the long run you're the winner. Frequently, the other side will be more willing to give concessions if they see you're serious about walking away or saying no to a bad deal.

NINE WAYS TO FAIL AT NEGOTIATING

Read through and discuss each item below. Compare each negotiating taboo with taboos in your country.

1) **Ignore the marketplace.** Everyone wants to buy low and sell high. If you insist on paying less than market value, you will either never be able to buy anything or you will end up buying something that was not of value in the first place.

2) **Don't listen.** Most of us assume the other side wants to take away that which is most important to us. Listening carefully to the other side's position often allows you to solve their problem at a very low cost to you.

3) **Concentrate on disagreements.** It is tempting to go straight to the problem in the deal. This creates a deadlock. Start with and emphasize the points of agreement, no matter how small. This gives the other side hope that compromise is possible on the big issues.

4) **Take unreasonable positions.** Unreasonable positions create distrust and distrust ruins deals. When something is overpriced, for example, the buyer wonders what is wrong with the business. On the other hand, if a buyer offers a lowball offer, the seller may feel insulted and angry.

5) **Delay.** Time is the enemy of every deal. We all have second thoughts about committing ourselves. As time goes by, we are more likely to think that we might be making a mistake.

6) **Treat the other party as an enemy.** People want to do business with people they like. Listening to the other side will often help you get a better and an easier deal. Making enemies will get you a lack of cooperation.

7) **Negotiate against yourself.** Good negotiators will ask you to do better before they respond to your last position. Don't fall for it!

8) **Make continuous counteroffers.** Some people can't quit when they are ahead. Dragging out the negotiations with multiple counteroffers decreases the chance of ever reaching a friendly agreement.

9) **Don't put things in writing.** This is the most common negotiating mistake. All deals must be put in black and white. Misunderstandings occur easily. Never let a deal fall through because something wasn't put in writing.

WIN-WIN NEGOTIATING

As you have learned from the previous pages, in negotiating there does not need to be one winner and one loser. Both sides can win and both sides can maintain a strong relationship. Match the headings with the most suitable information to create a page on positive Win-Win Negotiating.

Headings	*Information*
1) Find Out Who Has the Advantage	_____ Be prepared to compromise; give up what you don't need if the other party needs it.
2) Research the Other Party	_____ Be consistent, honest, accurate, and sincere. Once you lose your credibility, it is extremely hard to regain it.
3) Begin on a Positive Note	_____ Don't talk around the subject. Look for "non-verbal" signs of communication.
4) Agree on an Outcome	_____ When the discussion gets heated, be very careful not to get personal or to place blame. Deal with concrete subjects and issues.
5) Stay Focused	_____ Use exact dates and deadlines instead of vague phrases such as "as soon as possible."
6) Communicate Directly	_____ Try to arrive at an "upbeat" or positive conclusion, especially if the negotiations were heated.
7) Focus on Both Parties' Needs	_____ Ask yourself, "Who needs the other more?" Who has more time to wait if necessary? Who has more information?
8) Don't Get Personal	_____ Say something to create a positive atmosphere and to reduce tension when you first start.
9) Don't Play Negotiating Games	_____ Never use manipulation, force, games, or non-verbal tricks such as uncomfortable facial expressions or body movements.
10) Be Explicit and Concrete	_____ Find out as much as possible about the other party. What are their needs? What is their style? What method of communicating with them will be most effective?
11) Be Willing to Compromise	_____ Let the other party know that there can be a win-win outcome. Let them know that there can be benefits for both parties.
12) Guard Your Credibility	_____ Stick to the subject, the facts, and the issues. Don't focus on irrelevant matters.
13) End on a Positive Note	_____ Identify the other party's needs and do what you can to fulfill them. The other party should try to do the same for you.

FILL-IN-THE-BLANKS

Fill in the blanks in the following paragraphs using the words listed before each part of the article, Keep A Good Attitude. **Then read and discuss the article as a class.**

KEEP A GOOD ATTITUDE

negotiating	*strategies*	*efforts*	*outcome*
game	*successful*	*attitude*	*sides*

Your_____and behavior can affect the_____of many things in your life, including negotiations. When_____, a win-win philosophy is most profitable. A_____negotiation process results in both_____feeling like they have gained something for their_____. Objectives,_____, and tactics are only part of the negotiation_____.

respect	*needs*	*desires*	*sensitive*
compromise	*Empathy*	*long-term*	*negotiation*

You need to be_____to the_____of others. Being empathetic can gain the _____of others and create a_____business relationship with the other party. _____implies that you are trying to see the needs, wants, and_____through the eyes of the other person. You need to be willing to_____. An uncompromising position will leave you closed to creative ideas. In a win-win situation, the words_____and compromise are synonymous.

unusual	*problem*	*idea*	*Conflict*	*role plays*
confidence	*skills*	*solution*	*Develop*	*process*

_____your creative problem-solving_____. Don't be afraid to voice an idea that is _____. Your unusual_____may turn out to be the best _____to the_____. Learn to welcome conflict._____is a natural part of the negotiation_____. Practice resolving conflict situations in_____with friends and co-workers. This practice will give you more_____at the negotiation table.

angry	*behavior*	*temper*	*stressful*	*win-win*

Be patient. Losing your_____is a sign that you are losing your_____attitude. Take a break if you find yourself becoming_____. Negotiating can be_____. Still, don't let the actions of others determine your_____.

listen	importance	homework	misunderstandings
understood	Improve	assertive	remember

_____your listening skills by paraphrasing what the other party is saying to avoid
_____. The more you_____, the more you will understand and be

_____.

Do your_____before the start of the negotiation meeting to make sure you know the
_____of each issue.

Be_____, not aggressive._____, the harder you push, the harder the other party will
push back.

Negotiating Joke

While a hunter was in the woods, he took aim at a bear. The bear said, "Hold on; let's negotiate and see if we can get this problem worked out."

"Okay," said the hunter.

The bear continued, "What do you want?"

The hunter replied, "I want a fur coat. What do you want?"

The bear said, "I want a full stomach."

So they worked things out. The hunter got a fur coat and the bear got a full stomach.

MORAL: What is the moral of this story?

MAXIMS

Below is a sampling of maxims, or sayings, that may be helpful to remember in a negotiating session. Think how each one might compare with those used in your country.

Make your bargain before beginning to plow.   --Arab Proverb

First learn the meaning of what you say, and only then speak.   --Epictetus

Many things are lost for want of asking.   --George Herbert

Once you consent to some concessions, you can never
cancel it and put things back the way they are.   --Howard Hughes

You should not convey to an opponent, either by word or action,
that you want whatever the opponent has.   --John Illich

It is better to give away the wool than the sheep.   --Italian proverb

Let us never negotiate out of fear. But let us never fear to negotiate.   --John F. Kennedy

The fellow that agrees with everything you say is either
a fool or is getting ready to skin you.   --Henry L. Mencken

If you think you have someone eating out of your hand,
it's a good idea to count your fingers.   --Martin Buxbaum

To obtain a just compromise, concession must not only be mutual--
it must be equal also...There can be no hope that either will
yield more than it gets in return.   --John Marshall

NEGOTIATING MONETARY ITEMS

In this exercise the class will be divided 2 by 2 into Employers and Employees. The employers will try to maintain as much of the present system as possible and the employees will try to negotiate to get as many of their requests as possible. Both sides are flexible and willing to negotiate. This is not a hostile (unfriendly) situation. Encourage students to use the positive methods and avoid the negative methods explained in the previous pages.

Negotiating Topic	What is the Present System?	What is the Requested Change?
Base Pay	_____	_____
Overtime Pay	_____	_____
Bonus	_____	_____
Holiday Pay	_____	_____
Retirement Plan	_____	_____
	_____	_____
	_____	_____
Health Insurance	_____	_____
Mileage Allowance	_____	_____
Commissions	_____	_____

NEGOTIATING NON-MONETARY BENEFITS

Negotiating Topic	_What is the Present System?_	_What is the Requested Change?_
Sick Leave	_____	_____
Personal Leave	_____	_____
Maternity Leave	_____	_____
Comp Time	_____	_____
Paid Vacations	_____	_____
Flex Time	_____	_____
Telecommuting	_____	_____

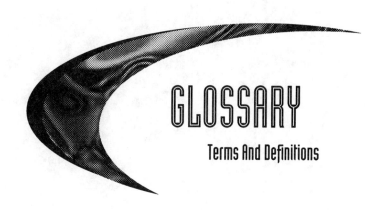

GLOSSARY

Terms And Definitions

abundance — plenty
acceptable — O.K.
access — a way in; ability to enter
accountable — being responsible for something or someone
accountant — one trained in keeping records of money going in and out of a company
adapt — to change or adjust
administrator — a person in a responsible position
advantage — benefit or gain
advent — the point in time that marks a beginning
aggressive — having force or energy
airmail — mail carried by plane
allotment — a portion or share
analyze — to study
applicant — one who is requesting something
application — a form used by an applicant to make his or her request
appreciation — an expression of gratitude; an increase in net worth
appropriate — proper or correct
approximately — about; nearly
architect — a person who designs buildings
assemble — to put or gather together
assign — to appoint to a post or position
assumption — belief in something not yet proven
authority — right; power
automation — making something work on its own
avoid — to keep away from

backbone — strongest area; foundation
bankrupt — financial ruin
based — placed or located in a specific area
beforehand — in advance; ahead of time
benefits — advantages or special gains
Better Business Bureau — consumer protection organization which monitors businesses
bid — an offer made to acquire something
blue collar worker — a physical laborer (one who uses his or her muscles on the job)
board — committee or organization of leaders

boasting — drawing attention to oneself; bragging
bottom line — final or end result; profit or loss
branch — a separate but dependent part of a company
brutal — unfeeling; harsh; ruthless
budget — (n) a plan for spending; (v) the creation of a plan for spending
bulletin board — a place where messages are put for others to see
bureau — an organization
bureaucracy — government groups
bureaucrat — a government official

C.O.D — cash on delivery
calling card — telephone "credit card"
candid — honest; frank; free from bias
capital hungry — needing money
cartel — businesses that work together to limit competition
cashier — a person who collects money from customers
cellular phone — telephone that uses satellite
CEO — Chief Executive Officer (often a company's president)
chain of command — order of authority in an organization
chairman — a presiding or administering officer
Chamber of Commerce — group of businessmen in a city that encourage business growth
channel — a line of communication or procedure for completing a goal
chauvinist — one who is excessively connected to an idea or cause
collaboration — working together
colleague — a fellow worker
collect call — telephone call paid for by the receiver of the call
commodity — something useful or valuable
compensate — to replace a loss; an exchange of equal value
compromise — to meet halfway in order to agree
compulsory — mandatory; without choice
computerization — to change from man to computer operated
conference — a formal meeting or discussion
conservative — relying on tradition
consult — to ask advice or opinions of someone

consumer	one who buys and / or uses a product
contractor	a person who agrees (in writing) to do or provide something
copyright	the authority to withhold permission to "copy" literally or figuratively
cordial	very sincere; from the heart
corporate structure	how a business is organized
criteria	a standard or set of rules
critical	to find fault with something
currency	money

databanks	collection of information
deadline	the time at which something must be completed
decline	to decrease in value; to say no to (an offer)
decrease	to lessen in value
deduct	to subtract from
define	to make clear; give definition to
department	a section or division of a company
depreciation	a loss of original value
deregulation	to remove governing rules (most commonly in reference to government removing its control over something)
destination	end of journey or project
detail	a specific part
develop	to make, create, build or add to
dilemma	a problem
diligence	hard work
directory assistance	operator paid to help customers locate phone numbers
disastrous	(adj) sudden misfortune
discrimination	prejudicial treatment
dismiss	to permit or cause to leave
disrupt	to cause disorder
diversify	to expand upon a company's original products or services
diversion	pastime; amusement
dues	money paid for membership to a group
duty	responsibility

earn	to receive payment or reward for work
enclosure	that which is included with a letter
engineer	a person who runs or supervises a machine
entrepreneur	a person who builds and runs a business
environment	conditions of an area
environmentalist	one who develops methods to improve the environment
establish	to bring into existence
estimate	to give a reasonable guess
etiquette	manners prescribed by custom which explain proper behavior in social situations
exclusive	limited possession, control or use
executive	a person in upper management
expand	to make larger
explicitly	(adj) clearly, without question
express	quickly

facade	a false or artificial showing
fax	(n) letter sent via telephone lines; machine used to send such letters (v) to send via fax machine
firm	a business or company; unbending
flexible	able to change easily
forbidden	not allowed, against the rules
foreman	one who oversees specific people
form letter	letter containing similar information yet addressed to different people
formal	following a strict set of rules and customs
forum	a public meeting or group of people
foster	to work with a plan or idea (to see it develop)
fragile	easily breakable
frustrated	discouraged, upset
fundamental	basic, standard
funding	money for a specific purpose

generally · usually; in most cases
gradually · little by little; a bit at a time
grapevine · a "person-to-person" means of spreading information

halt · to stop
hands off · indirect; letting someone work on their own
hands on · working directly with a person
harmony · agreement of feeling
headquarters · the main office of a business

illegal · against the law
illustrate · to show an idea by use of examples
impolite · without manners
in charge · responsible for seeing that work gets done
incentives · that which is intended to provide motivation for greater performance
indicate · to tell or inform
informal · ordinary, casual; familiar
innovation · something new;
invent · to create for the first time
irrelevant · not important; not related

join · to bring together
joint venture · two or more parties working together on a project

Laizzez-Faire · a "hands off" attitude or policy
"leads" · possible business connections

letterhead · statement of name, address and other information on company stationery
liberalize · to free from restrictions
literacy · ability to read and write
logo · an emblem used to represent a company

maintain · to take care of regularly
maitre d' · the host of a restaurant
major · largest; most important
manila folders · large envelopes used to mail documents without folding them
manipulate · to change or control by unfair means to work to ones own advantage
manufacture · to produce a product
market strategies · tactics used in selling
market survey · a study of the public's opinion regarding a product or service
meager · insufficient; not enough; a little
memorandum · (memo); a written note
merchandising · promoting the sale of goods
middleman · a person who works in-between a producer and the seller of a product
mingle · to mix together (usually applies to people "mingling" with other people
minimum · the smallest amount possible
mislead · to give the wrong idea
modernization · changing something old or out of date by applying current technology
monopoly · complete control, ownership or command of supply
mortgage · an agreement to repay a loan
motto · a short phrase used to express an idea
multinational · represented by or located in many different countries

negotiations · talking together to make a deal
network · (v) to get information from others
nominated · chosen or appointed
notation · a character, abbreviation or symbol

objective	a goal
observe	to notice, watch
obstacle	something standing in the way of progress or improvement
ordinarily	usually; most of the time
overhead	cost of doing business (rent, wages, supplies etc.)

partnership	two people sharing work
patent	government recognition of a product's original inventor
paycheck	the check used to pay employees
pension	a fixed amount of money paid to a person after retiring from a company
personnel	employees
philosophy	general beliefs; ideas
plush	luxurious
policy	definite course or method of action
polite	well mannered
post card	a card needing no envelope to be handled by the post office
postage	amount of money needed to send mail
postmark	mark on envelope indicating that mail has been through the postal system
potentially	possibly
prejudice	feelings against someone or something
prestigious	honored, highly regarded
primary	most basic, most important
prior	before; earlier in time
process	a set way of doing something
profit	money remaining after all overhead is paid out
prompt	on time
proposal	suggestion; offer
proprietorship	legal right or title to something
punctual	on time, prompt

qualified	to be skilled in a certain field
quality control	system of product testing to ensure high quality
quitting time	end of the work day

rarely	seldom; not common
raw material	yet unworked supplies (i.e., wood, earth metals, coal, etc.)
real estate	land and buildings
reap	to receive payment; obtain; win
recession	a period of reduced economic activity
reference	a person who can verify what has been said by someone else
regulations	rules that govern business
rejects	products that do not meet quality standards
request	to ask for something
response	answer
retailer	a person who sells to the public
retire	to stop working (usually due to age)
revenue	money received on an investment
revolutionize	to completely change
rigorously	strict, severely
roundtable	a discussion held by several people
rude	not polite

S.A.S.E	self addressed stamped envelope
salary	wage given for a job
salary schedule	set payment based on specific guidelines (usually seniority, education and job performance)
sales division	the department of a business that manages the sales of products and services
sales force	the workers in the sales division
salutation	a greeting (usually in a letter)

sample	a small example of a product
securities	evidence of ownership of stocks or bonds
security	safety, freedom from fear or worry
seniority	a position of status obtained by working for a company for a long time
set up	to arrange or prepare to use
severely	strictly; harshly
sexist	prejudice against women or men
shareholder	one who owns company stock
shun	to keep or turn away from
signature	a person's self-written name
simila	alike in many ways
skyrocket	to increase very rapidly
solve	to find an answer
spawn	to expand, increase or spread out
specialty	distinctive mark or expertise
speculation	making a bid in hopes of a high return
spouse	husband or wife
staff	key workers in a business venture
staggered	uneven; overlapping
standstill	no movement; stop
start-up costs	money needed to begin a business (venture capital)
stationary	high quality paper used for letters
statistics	collection of information
stock	partial right of ownership sold by companies in order to raise capital
stockholder	one who owns company stock
strategy	organization and plan of action
strict	severe; harsh
strike	work stoppage by employees refusing to work in order to have their demands met
subcontractor	a party that agrees to fill all or part of another party's contract
subsidiary	a company controlled by another company
sufficient	enough
suitable	useful for what is needed
supervisor	one who oversees others
supplement	(n) something added; (v) to add
supplier	one who sells supplies
supremacy	highest in power
surplus	more than needed; excess
systematic	in an orderly manner; methodical

tactic	a method used to accomplish something
tariff	taxes placed on imported and exported products
task	work that is assigned
technology	technical method of achieving a practical purpose
teller	a bank clerk
test	to try out; to use
totalitarian	relating to centralized control by an autocratic (complete authority) leader
touch tone	type of telephone that produces a specific "tone" for each number pressed
transaction	a business deal or agreement
trend	a general movement; a current style
typical	symbolic; distinctive

unfamiliar	not well known; strange
union leader	highest authority in a labor union
U.S. Department of Commerce	U.S. government trade department

various	many different kinds
via	"by way of" or "by means of"
viable	capable of growing or developing
vice president	second in charge or authority
vital	necessary

watchman	a guard at a company/building
white collar worker	office worker
wholesaler	a middleman who sells to merchants
willingness	desire to act or respond by choice

Yellow Pages	business directory of a phone book